VIRGILIO ELIZONDO

MODERN SPIRITUAL MASTERS SERIES

VIRGILIO ELIZONDO

Spiritual Writings

Selected with an Introduction by

TIMOTHY MATOVINA

ORBIS BOOKS

Maryknoll, New York 10545

Founded in 1970, Orbis Books endeavors to publish works that enlighten the mind, nourish the spirit, and challenge the conscience. The publishing arm of the Maryknoll Fathers and Brothers, Orbis seeks to explore the global dimensions of the Christian faith and mission, to invite dialogue with diverse cultures and religious traditions, and to serve the cause of reconciliation and peace. The books published reflect the views of their authors and do not represent the official position of the Maryknoll Society. To learn more about Maryknoll and Orbis Books, please visit our website at www.maryknollsociety.org.

Library of Congress Cataloging-in-Publication Data

Elizondo, Virgilio P.
    Virgilio Elizondo : spiritual writings / selected with an introduction by Timothy Matovina.
        p. cm.
    Includes bibliographical references.
    ISBN 978-1-57075-865-2 (pbk.)
        1. Spirituality – Catholic Church. 2. Catholic Church – Doctrines.
    3. Hispanic American theology. 4. Elizondo, Virgilio P., 1935-   I. Matovina, Timothy M., 1955-   II. Title.
    BX2350.65.E45 2010
    248.4'8208968 – dc22   2009036500

Do you want to see, understand, and appreciate Jesus today?
I cannot think of a better way than to enter into the lives
of those who are living similar experiences and struggles today,
those living in the "Galilees" of today's world,
those living in the margins and crossroads.

— Virgilio Elizondo, *A God of Incredible Surprises*

Contents

Preface

Readers of this anthology should know I am not a casual observer of Virgilio Elizondo's writings; my familiarity with Virgilio and his work is indicated throughout this collection by the use of his first name. I first met Virgilio in 1982 when I was his student at the Mexican American Cultural Center in San Antonio. Our friendship and collaboration have been deepening ever since. We have written and edited books together, collaborated on numerous presentations and projects, and to the present team teach courses at the University of Notre Dame.

Virgilio's friends and colleagues from far and wide and our students at Notre Dame graciously accepted the invitation to contribute their insights and critical observations to drafts of this manuscript. I am grateful to all of them: Michael Anthony Abril, María Pilar Aquino, Matthew Ashley, Jacques Audinet, Sofia Barbato, Kevin Burke, S.J., Davíd Carrasco, Víctor Carmona, Janet Diaz, Mary Doak, Eduardo Fernández, S.J., Terry Garza, Eduardo González, Michelle González, Daniel Groody, C.S.C., Michael Lee, Monica Mata, Jeanette Rodriguez, Christopher Tirres, Neto Valiente, and Barbara Winston. Series editor Robert Ellsberg and his colleagues at Orbis Books provided, as always, kind and expert companionship in developing the manuscript. A special word of thanks to Cushwa Center student assistants John Aversa, Brian Sarnacki, Zander Stachniak, and Francys Verdial Argueta, and to Paula Brach for her various and typically outstanding contributions to editorial and production matters.

I also acknowledge with gratitude the publishers, journals, and organizations that granted permissions to reprint excerpts from Virgilio's writings, as well as all the editors and colleagues who oversaw the original publication venues for the selections that appear in this anthology: Catholic News Service, Catholic Television of San Antonio, Catholic Theological Society of America, College Theology Society, *Concilium,* Judson Press, *Listening: Journal of Religion and Culture,* Orbis Books, *Origins,* Our Sunday Visitor, Paulist Press, Rowman and Littlefield, St. Anthony Messenger Press, *San Antonio Express, SEDOS —* Service of Documentation and Study on Global Mission, *Theological Studies,* Twenty-Third Publications, University Press of Colorado, and *The Way: Contemporary Christian Spirituality.*

Virgilio Elizondo is an esteemed mentor, colleague, and friend. I have been presenting his writings to pastoral leaders and students for nearly three decades. It was a joy to read them anew in the preparation of this anthology. My prayer for you as reader is that his spiritual wisdom will enlighten you as it has me and many others.

Introduction

In every age, the church carries the responsibility of reading the signs of the times and of interpreting them in the
light of the Gospel.   — *Gaudium et Spes,* no. 4

Virgilio Elizondo grew up in the Mexican American neighborhoods on the west side of San Antonio, where his parents had
met after fleeing their homeland during the violence of the Mexican Revolution. A San Antonio diocesan priest for nearly half a
century, he was ordained during the years of the Second Vatican
Council and became fascinated with the conciliar documents
and vision, especially the call for a return to the sources of
faith. Following this directive of the Council, Virgilio's writings and pastoral leadership reexamine two foundational faith
sources: the Jesus stories of the Gospels and the image and
apparitions narrative of Our Lady of Guadalupe. He has often
remarked that his Mexican Catholic upbringing grounded his
faith and his spiritual reflections in these celestial companions:
Jesus of Nazareth, "suffering for us on the cross and with us in
our struggles," and Our Lady of Guadalupe, "reigning majesti-
cally in the temple of our hearts while offering us all her love,
defense, and protection."[1] His meditations name the ugliness of
sin and the beauty of redeemed humanity in a language that is
deeply rooted both in contemporary human reality and in God's
saving power revealed in Jesus of Galilee and proclaimed in the
Americas through Our Lady of Guadalupe. Virgilio responds to
the call all Christians have received: to proclaim the one Gospel
of Jesus Christ in fresh ways such that it takes flesh as good
news in the times and places of our lives.

Though Virgilio is widely renowned as a theologian, like
other volumes in this Modern Spiritual Masters series the focus

11

of this anthology is not primarily on his theological contributions, nor on the theological investigations, debates, and further
insights his work has inspired. The purpose of this book is
twofold: (1) to explore Virgilio's life and faith as the spiritual
core that animates his pastoral and theological work and (2) to
make his spiritual wisdom and writings accessible to an even
wider readership than the many who have already benefited
from his publications and presentations.

Spirituality precedes theology, which in its classical definition — "faith seeking understanding" — presumes that the one
theologizing has already experienced God and is now seeking
a deeper understanding of that experience and its implications.
Theology occurs in a second moment. The encounter with God
comes first. But this does not reduce spirituality to some private
feeling about ourselves and our relationship with God. Virgilio's
writings illuminate spirituality as a fundamental relationship we
have, through a gift, with God and with Our Lady of Guadalupe, the saints, and one another. This gift is mediated through
community, culture, and church. Spirituality is about deepening relationships with God and our neighbor, especially the
marginal peoples who resiliently acclaim God's love for them
even as they question and confront unjust suffering. Consistent with these convictions, this introductory essay highlights
an approach to theology as spiritual discernment that Virgilio
developed in his first book publication and in his first major
works on the Galilean Jesus and on Guadalupe. He extended
this approach in his subsequent writings, excerpts of which are
examined in the body of this work to collectively present his
foundational spiritual insights.

Who Is Virgilio Elizondo?

Virgilio is an internationally acclaimed pastor and theologian.
He is widely renowned as the founder of U.S. Latino theol-
ogy. In 1972 he established the Mexican American Cultural
Center (MACC, now the Mexican American Catholic College),

a distinguished theological think tank and training center for pastoral leaders among Mexican Americans and other Latinas and Latinos in the United States. He has lectured and taught throughout the Western hemisphere and on every continent. His numerous honors include being named one of *Time* magazine's spiritual innovators for the new millennium, eight honorary doctorates, the John Courtney Murray Award for outstanding theological contributions from the Catholic Theological Society of America, the Johannes Quasten Award for excellence and leadership in theological development from the Catholic University of America, the Humanitarian Award of the National Conference of Christians and Jews, and the Laetare Medal from the University of Notre Dame, the oldest and most prestigious award for American Catholics, given to honorees whose lives exemplify a distinctively Catholic contribution to humanity. Virgilio's colleagues in the Academy of Catholic Hispanic Theologians of the United States (ACHTUS) recognized his status as the premier Latino theologian by founding the Virgilio Elizondo Award, a prize given to an honoree for "outstanding contributions to a theology of and for U.S. Hispanics." He has authored more than a dozen books, two dozen edited volumes, and over a hundred articles. As rector of San Fernando Cathedral in San Antonio, Texas, from 1983 to 1995 he led the effort to revitalize the parish as a center of public ritual and traditions and inaugurated the weekly bilingual Misa de las Américas that he arranged to have televised from San Fernando to viewers throughout the United States and beyond. He joined the faculty at the University of Notre Dame in 1999, where he continues to teach as the Notre Dame Professor of Pastoral and Hispanic Theology and Fellow of the Institute for Latino Studies. Yet he continues to commute from his primary residence in San Antonio, where he directs programming initiatives with Catholic Television of San Antonio and serves as parochial vicar of St. Rose of Lima parish.

The most direct and persistent influence of Virgilio's theological reflection, pastoral action, and activism has been in

Hispanic ministry and theology. He was a catalyst for many of the changes in Hispanic ministry in the United States over the past four decades, particularly the prophetic insistence that pastoral leaders respect Hispanic faith expressions and cultures. But his influence is limited neither to Latinos nor to the borders of the United States. He has served on the editorial board of the *Revista Latinoamericana de Teología* and participated prominently in the Ecumenical Association of Third World Theologians (EATWOT), a group he commends for enabling theologians from across the globe to support and enrich one another in "today's struggles for liberation, whether that of a Hispanic in the U.S.A., a Zimbabwean in Africa, an untouchable in India, or an Aymara in Peru."[2] From 1979 to 1999 he also served on the editorial board of *Concilium,* a widely acclaimed publication that arguably is as much an international forum for theological and ecclesial renewal as it is a theological journal. He co-edited over a dozen volumes of *Concilium* with international authors on topics ranging from pilgrimage to the option for the poor to the reception and understanding of Christ in Asia.

Yet beyond his many accolades and impressive accomplishments lies what most consider a full, blessed, but relatively inconspicuous life: the firm foundation of a good family upbringing, seminary training and ordination, ministry as a priest and teacher, leadership in the Mexican American struggles for dignity and justice, speaking and writing on his journey of discipleship. Virgilio does not write about extraordinary occurrences but, like many spiritual writers, he seeks to find the extraordinary in the ordinary. As will be evident throughout this anthology, beginning with the first chapter, which presents an autobiographical sketch of Virgilio's life, the heart of his spiritual writing is unveiling Gospel dynamics in "common" lives and everyday events.

First and foremost Virgilio is a pastor. His initial assignment as a priest was to Our Lady of Sorrows parish in San Antonio, and he has served in some form of parochial ministry ever since. His teaching, writing, lecturing, video productions, and other work are all rooted in and enhance the pastoral core of his life and ministry. Having served as a priest among predominantly working-class Mexican Americans for nearly half a century, Virgilio has learned from his parishioners and from his own experience that one of the most pernicious effects of sin is the bruised self-esteem of those who suffer insults and rejection. Many of his parishioners have stinging memories of the polite disdain or outright hostility they met in their dealings with sales clerks, bosses, coworkers, teachers, police officers, health care providers, social workers, government employees, professional colleagues, and even church leaders. Virgilio frequently has noted that the pain many of his people endure is fundamentally rooted in their living in between cultures and not being fully accepted, either as Mexicans among their counterparts born in the land of their ancestors or as U.S. Americans among their fellow residents in the place they call home. The pain of rejection can be so severe and so deeply internalized that many doubt their fundamental goodness as daughters and sons of God. These realities led Virgilio to the Gospel mandates at the heart of his preaching, teaching, and writings: he persistently and passionately invites his hearers — be they Mexican Americans or people of any other background — to discover in the Scriptures and in their own religious traditions the core message that God cherishes us, loves us, and calls us to confront the forces of sinful rejection in ourselves and in the world around us.

The Human Quest

A seminarian when Pope John XXIII announced he would convene the Second Vatican Council, Virgilio followed the Council with great fascination and has engaged its teachings and its vision ever since. Though commentators continue to debate the proper interpretation of Vatican II, Virgilio reminds us that the Council is not only a collection of documents and official teachings but more profoundly a providential and ecclesial event that animates us to deepen our commitment to Christ and the church. In this sense the foundation of Virgilio's writings are the meditations of a pastor and theologian who decided to take Vatican II seriously. One mandate of the Council that deeply influenced him was the encouragement for the church to turn toward the world, so that it could more fully engage the joys and hopes as well as the questions and challenges humanity faces today. The council fathers urged the members of the church to scrutinize the signs of the times and interpret those signs in light of the Gospel. In other words, Catholics are to examine the conditions in which people live, seek to discern how those conditions reflect or contradict the will of God, and work to transform our lives and our surroundings to make them more harmonious with God's redeeming plan.

Virgilio joined pastors and theologians around the globe who responded to this call in varied attempts to articulate the context in which they are doing pastoral ministry and theology, that is, the human situation to which they are responding with the Word of God and Christian tradition. Rather than beginning with the revealed truths of the faith and then applying them to Christian living, a procedure common in classical theology, this approach starts with an explicit attempt to analyze people's daily reality. The presumption of those employing this approach is that we must uncover the significance of Christian revelation for very particular times, places, and people, lest the Christian message become a mere platitude devoid of meaning in everyday life. While the faith is one, the ways of articulating it to bring it alive within the diverse contexts of our world are many.

Virgilio's writings have consistently contributed to the collective effort of concretely naming beauty, sin, and suffering as the first step to discerning a Christian response in light of the Gospel. But assessing the human situation is by no means a simple process of observation, of course. Our perceptions of human joys, pains, and longings are inherently subjective judgments.

Trained observers are attentive not just to what they are seeing, but also to themselves as the ones who are doing the "seeing." No one is a neutral observer. All of us assess the world around us through the lens of our preconceived notions and biases. For Christians this includes our understanding of the Gospel message and what it demands of us. Virgilio's use of anecdote and autobiographical voice in his early writings increased over the following decades as he articulated more and more clearly the particular life context out of which his spiritual insights emerge.

Embracing Vatican II's challenge to respond to the sign of the times, in his writings Virgilio adopts the see-judge-act approach that Belgian Cardinal Joseph Cardijn, founder of the Young Christian Workers, developed and popularized. Virgilio's first book, *A Search for Meaning in Life and Death* (1971), employs a three-part organizational structure that established the pattern of these steps for subsequent publications: attempting to see reality, judge it in light of the Gospels, and act to transform it accordingly. While the written page necessarily presents these three steps in linear fashion, however, in fact the process is far more dynamic. Even as we "see" we already have conceptions of how we will "judge" and "act." In this first book and throughout his writings, Virgilio illuminates this dynamism, presenting the three steps sequentially for the sake of clarity but also interweaving elements of each into the other parts of the book to show their mutual interrelations.

The introduction for *A Search for Meaning in Life and Death* states that the "primary purpose for this work is to develop a catechesis for twentieth-century adult Christians seeking to deepen their understanding and appreciation of their faith."[3] He cites various sources that shaped the work, such as the ideas of contemporary thinkers like Pierre Teilhard de Chardin and Karl Rahner, his experiences with Latin American theologians and leaders of the East Asian Pastoral Institute in Manila, and especially Vatican II. Yet the starting point of the work, the first paragraph in the first chapter of his first major publication, does not enunciate any revealed theological truth but, echoing some of these foundational sources such as Vatican II's *Gaudium et Spes* (Pastoral Constitution on the Church in the Modern World), no. 10, poses the question of the riddle of human existence:

> From our earliest years, we begin to ask questions. As we grow, we seek to know the meaning of the realities that we encounter around us; increasingly, our questions become more penetrating. We begin to discover our uniqueness. We become aware that we are conscious, and begin to ask the meaning of this consciousness. Who am I? What is life? Why am I here?[4]

Reflecting an awareness of poverty rooted in his context as a Mexican American pastor serving among poor and working-class parishioners, Virgilio quickly adds in the very next lines of his exposition that these life questions are asked from different perspectives, contrasting the person "who is sitting in his comfortable den enjoying a drink after a successful day" with the one "who is facing the end of another day without money to buy the necessary drugs for his sick child." As he often does throughout his corpus of writings, he roots his analyses in a key text of the Second Vatican Council: "In language intelligible to every generation, it [the church] should be able to answer the ever recurring questions which people ask about the meaning of this present life and of the life to come, and how one is related to the other" (*Gaudium et Spes,* no. 4).

The attempt to "see" the situation of humans in the modern world continues throughout part 1 of the book. On the one hand, Virgilio observes various pitfalls of contemporary existence and poignantly asks why there is such great "emptiness in the lives of so many people today?"[5] He probes the sources of evil and destructiveness that plague humanity. Sin is born in pride and egoism and then seems to take on a devastating life of its own. Human failure can appear so acute that he even provocatively entitles one chapter "Humanity: A Mistake of the Gods?" On the other hand, in a moving meditation on the origins of the human species and the genesis of religious thought, Virgilio delineates a fundamental conviction that runs through his writings: every human person radiates beauty, dignity, and the innate capacity for faith and heroic goodness. Here the influence of the visionary Jesuit paleontologist, biologist, and philosopher Pierre Teilhard de Chardin (1881–1955) on Virgilio is evident. Though cited only occasionally in Virgilio's later writings, Teilhard de Chardin's contemplation of the wonder of human life, especially his renowned book *The Phenomenon of Man,* grounds Virgilio's insistence about the dignity and beauty of each human person as well as Virgilio's deep convictions about God's cosmic design to redeem not only humanity but all of creation.[6]

As Christians we judge the simultaneous human inclinations for hope and despair, for holiness and corruption, in light of God's revelation in salvation history. Virgilio engages this task of judging in part 2 of *A Search for Meaning in Life and Death.* He underscores that the incarnation, "this journey of God from the everlasting into the transitory — this leap into human history — is something no human intellect can comprehend" and observes that many "are still scandalized" at how very human God became in Christ.[7] In straightforward language, he contends that we find the answer to the riddle of our everyday human existence in our contemplation of the totality of the Christ event. One memorable passage links Jesus to our everyday struggles and challenges:

> The poet takes the simple, everyday syllables of language, and Jesus also took the simple, everyday elements of life: soil, the seed, water, work, rest, and found a place for them in His message. Through Him the elements of life become notes and chords in a new symphony. He took people just as they were: tax collectors receiving bribes; the crusted, cursing, stinking fishermen; or the clean-cut young man — sinner or saints. He helped them find the beauty, joy, and strength of unfailing love in daily life.[8]

If the purpose and destiny of human life are unfathomable mysteries, the mystery of God becoming human for us is even more inscrutable. Jesus reveals to us both the truth about God and the truth about the human. The glory of God is revealed in human beings who are alive in Christ. Thus as Christians we must judge our everyday life possibilities and choices against the fullness of human life God has revealed in Christ.

The final part of the book urges the reader to act on the call to follow Christ in the face of suffering and death and in the desire for fulfillment inscribed in our human experience. Virgilio enjoins his hearers to struggle against evils — hunger and crime, poor housing and unjust wages, the excessive pursuit of pleasure and material comfort — while ever nurturing hope in the life beyond our earthly existence. He insists that Christianity is a "faith for the here-and-now," a vital option for people facing the dilemma of life in our modern world, a joyful pathway that "as preached by the Master, offers a new life, beginning here on earth, and perfected beyond the limits of time and space."[9]

Galilean Journey

The pattern of spiritual writing established in *A Search for Meaning in Life and Death* subsequently became even more embedded in the particularities of Virgilio's Mexican American experience. MACC was a major seedbed of this development, as through the 1970s it became the most creative center for Mexican Americans to think together about their life in church and society. These reflections led Virgilio and others to reject the notion that *mestizaje* — the dynamic and often violent mixing of cultures and peoples — was a curse that marked them as inferior. Instead Virgilio and his collaborators boldly embraced their heritage as *mestizos* born from two dramatic clashes: first Mesoamericans with the conquistadores of sixteenth-century Catholic Spain and then, in the century and a half following the U.S. takeover of northern Mexico, Mexican-descent residents with other peoples of the United States, including their fellow Catholics with European roots.

Virgilio consciously grounds his writings in his *mestizo* reality as a Mexican American pastor of the Texas-Mexico borderlands. Though others have categorized him as Hispanic or Latino and he himself embraces these identities insofar as they show his solidarity with other U.S. residents of Spanish-speaking ancestry, he insists that he would not be so presumptuous as to speak for the perspectives of Puerto Ricans, Cubans, El Salvadorans, Guatemalans, Dominicans, or other peoples who comprise the vastly diverse U.S. Hispanic population. Indeed, he does not even claim to speak for all other ethnic Mexicans in the United States, many of whom are recent immigrants, live in places other than Texas or the Southwest, are not Catholic, or have other characteristics and commitments that distinguish their experiences from those of Virgilio. The point of departure for Virgilio's writings is a quite particular one: the human situation of the Mexican American *mestizo* people of the borderlands and his reflections as a lifelong resident and Catholic pastor serving them in San Antonio.

This particularity of Virgilio's focus drew inspiration from the documents and vision of the Second Vatican Council, most notably *Ad Gentes,* the Decree on the Missionary Activity of the Church. Virgilio's writings cite this conciliar document more than any other, especially excerpts from article no. 22 such as the following:

> They [the young churches] borrow from the customs, traditions, wisdom, teaching, arts, and sciences of their people everything which could be used to praise the glory of the Creator, manifest the grace of the savior, or contribute to the right ordering of Christian life.
>
> To achieve this, it is necessary that in each of the great socio-cultural regions, as they are called, theological investigation should be encouraged and the facts and words

revealed by God, contained in sacred scripture, and explained by the fathers and magisterium of the church,
submitted to a new examination in the light of the tradition of the universal church.

Virgilio's spiritual writings and the founding vision of MACC
encompass this call to ground theological investigations in the
context of a particular sociocultural region and, within its
parameters, to examine anew the "words revealed by God."
Such analyses are not solely intended for the local communities
out of which they emerge. People of various backgrounds have
noted that Virgilio's spiritual and theological insights illuminate
their own faith and life experience. In the words of John Coleman, S.J., "Virgilio has taught us that it is precisely by being
deeply in touch with the particular that we also touch edges of
reality which resonate more universally."[10]

The life experiences of his Mexican American people led Virgilio to reexamine the transformative dynamics of the Gospel
narratives. His most acclaimed book is *Galilean Journey: The
Mexican-American Promise* (1983), a reworked and abbrevi-
ated version of his 1978 doctoral dissertation that was, as his
dissertation director Jacques Audinet so aptly put it, "a cultural
rereading of the Gospels, and a Gospel rereading of cultural
dynamics."[11] Once again this effort responded to a challenge
Virgilio found in the teachings of Vatican II:

> People will always be keen to know, if only in a general
> way, what is the meaning of their life, their activity, their
> death.... The most perfect answer to these questions is
> to be found in God alone, who created women and men
> in his own image and redeemed them from sin; and this
> answer is given in the revelation in Christ his Son who
> became man. To follow Christ the perfect human is to
> become more human oneself (*Gaudium et Spes,* no. 41).

Virgilio introduced *Galilean Journey* as "the story of the universal human quest as lived and expressed by the Mexican

American people of the Southwest U.S.A." and set as his primary objective enabling Mexican Americans to discover their "fundamental identity and mission" in the "acceptance and following of Jesus of Nazareth as the Lord of history and life."[12]

The first part of the book comprises Virgilio's efforts to see core elements of the history and contemporary experience of Mexican Americans. It begins with a summary of the conquests of central Mexico and then what became the Southwest United States, a historical process of subjugation that formed Mexican Americans as a *mestizo* people. This history exemplifies the dynamics of exclusion that often characterize human groups, unveiling the futile human tendencies to seek inner security through excluding and dehumanizing others. The impact of U.S. colonization continues in the pressures put on Mexican Americans to assimilate, to abandon the Mexican way for the U.S. American way. Tragically, the multiple ways a conquering or dominant group seeks to impose its own self-image as the standard of the good, the beautiful, and the human often rob the defeated of their fundamental sense that they too are sons and daughters made in God's own image.

Mexican American responses to assimilatory pressures have encompassed tactics for mere survival especially through isolation from the majority cultural group, efforts to "develop" into U.S. Americans, and attempts to confront the unwritten law that their culture must be abandoned. Most Mexican Americans engage in two or all three of these strategies, depending on the possibilities and limitations they face in particular situations of their daily lives. The third approach, which Virgilio calls "liberation movements," includes not only resistance to assimilation, but a communitarian vision that challenges the notion that unity can be realized only through uniformity. Mexican American religious traditions — especially those connected with the birth and death of Jesus and devotion to Our Lady of Guadalupe — fuel their life struggles with a sense of belonging, meaning, and hope in a God whose love and designs are far greater than the travails of their earthly existence.

Next Virgilio judges these perceptions of Mexican American realities against the Gospel narratives in an attempt to "look for areas of convergence and divergence" between the Gospel and the Mexican American situation and more fully enable "the way of Jesus to come alive in the faith community today."[13] This attempt is not solely aimed at applying the Gospel message to the contemporary situation. It is also, and simultaneously, an effort to pose questions out of the Mexican American experience that probe more deeply into the Gospel revelation. The Mexican American struggle for dignity and identity as *mestizos* who live between cultures led to *Galilean Journey*'s crucial question about Jesus' cultural identity, indeed the most central question in all of Virgilio's writings: Why did God become human as a Galilean? Since presumably God's Son could have been born in any time or place, what does his birth as a Galilean reveal about the meaning of the incarnation? Given that Galilee plays an exceedingly minor role in the Old Testament, why does the witness of the early Christians as recorded in the Gospels emphasize Jesus' origins as a Jew from Galilee? How does awareness of this emphasis deepen our understanding of the Gospels?

Even before Virgilio sets out to answer them, these questions comprise a major contribution to understanding the Gospels. Many preachers and writers speak of Jesus as if he were a generic human, detached from the specificities of a particular biological, cultural, and socioeconomic background. Virgilio teaches us that a key element of the incarnation is that God became human as a Galilean. Recognizing this core but often overlooked fact invites us to reexamine the Gospel proclamation of Jesus' life, from conception to resurrection, with vigilant recollection that the teacher, savior, and Lord we encounter, as well as the first followers he chose, were all Galileans. How does this recognition deepen our understanding of the mystery of what God has revealed in Christ?

Chapter 2 of this anthology explores Virgilio's response to this question in greater depth. He identifies Galilee as a marginal region whose inhabitants were often considered backward and impure. Jesus of Nazareth emerges from this land of the rejected as a teacher and healer whose words and deeds announce that God rejects no one. His table fellowship with all is a radical expression of God's all-encompassing love. Not limiting his compassion for the downtrodden to expressions of consolation, he goes to Jerusalem to confront the presumption that marginal Galileans, or any of God's children, are inherently impure. Though condemned to the horrific death of the cross, he condemns no one. Through forgiveness even of his persecutors he breaks the cycle of vengeance at the root of humanity's sinful and exclusionary tendencies. The resurrection not only vindicates his message, but inaugurates new life. Empowered in the Spirit on Pentecost, his Galilean followers announce the good news to people of diverse languages and cultures. What their Master began in Galilee will now spread to the far corners of the earth.

The final part of *Galilean Journey* is a call to the mission of discipleship, following Jesus from the rejection of Galilee to the confrontations of Jerusalem to the hope and new life of the resurrection. First Virgilio posits that God chooses the "Galileans" whom the world rejects. For *mestizos,* or anyone who has experienced the pain of rejection, the realization that God calls you is good news, indeed, the best news: I belong! I matter to someone, and not just to anyone, to God and to God's people! Those who have been transformed from the experience of rejection to election are in turn sent to announce the good news that God rejects no one. Like Jesus, their calling is not merely to comfort the afflicted, but to confront the "Jerusalems" of the contemporary world: "The disciples of Jesus cannot be content with welcoming others and doing good for others. They must join him in his struggle against the root and multiple causes of oppression. It is not sufficient to do good and avoid evil: the

disciple must do good and *struggle against* evil."[14] This struggle includes the confrontation with the sinful tendencies in our
own lives and immediate community and cultural group, as well
as those of others and the wider society. Christ's resurrection
instills our hope that God's love has the final say in this world,
and no human force can thwart God's designs.

Joyful celebrations of Christian life, from the Eucharist to the
fiestas prevalent among Mexican Americans and other believers,
are necessary complements to prophetic denunciation. Christian fiesta proclaims the new world that our faith assures us
has already begun to dawn in Christ's resurrection, even as it
witnesses to ongoing pain and tragedy and animates us to participate in Christ's redeeming work of transforming ourselves
and the world around us. "To those who have participated in
the collective mystical experience of Christian faith," Virgilio
avows, the fiestas of the poor and of authentic believers "are a
celebration of God's power unto new creation."[15] Thus to the
tripartite approach of see-judge-act Virgilio adds a vital fourth
step: celebrate. Especially for the marginal and the downtrodden, even as we act to transform our sinful ways and the sin of
the world around us, we are called to the joy of celebrating that
God is with us and God's presence inaugurates the new day for
which we long.

La Morenita

Devotions to the newborn and crucified Jesus and to Our Lady
of Guadalupe are the most foundational Mexican American celebrations of God's love animating their faith and hope amid
life's difficulties. Virgilio was the first U.S. Latino theologian to
write extensively on Guadalupe and explore the core meanings
of the fervent devotion to her. Implementing Vatican II's decree
that the church esteems and ennobles "whatever good is found
sown in people's hearts and minds, or in the rites and customs
of peoples" (*Lumen Gentium,* no. 17), he examines the Guadalupe encounter as a deeply inculturated proclamation of the

Gospel. His first book on the subject, *La Morenita: Evangelizer of the Americas* (1980), arose out of the dynamism of MACC, where he had examined Guadalupe in various workshop sessions and conversations over the previous decade. The volume has three parts: examining the historical context of Spanish conquest that impeded the evangelization process in sixteenth-century Mexico, judging violence and conquest in light of God's alternative announced through Guadalupe, and enacting the divine-human partnership to which the Guadalupe encounter beckons us.

As Virgilio says, widely divergent worldviews among Iberian Catholics and the Nahua or Aztec peoples of central Mexico only served to exacerbate Spanish designs to subdue the natives for profit and induce their conversion to Catholicism. Hernán Cortés led the forces that conquered the great Aztec capital of Tenochtitlan (now Mexico City) in 1521. In the wake of military victory, Spanish authorities attempted to destroy or alter all things indigenous: their political and economic systems, dress, customs, habits, language, and religion. Intentionally or not, as a consequence they also assailed the natives' sense of worth and purpose in life. While some missioners valiantly tried to buffer the atrocities of the conquest and preach the Gospel persuasively, Spanish violence against the native peoples seriously hindered their efforts. Virgilio deems the conquest nothing less than the violent meeting of two worlds, citing the desolate commentary of the Nahua wise ones who respectfully stated in a public colloquy with the first twelve Franciscans who came to evangelize them: "Allow us then to die, let us perish now, since our gods are already dead."[16]

In this context, Virgilio presents the Guadalupe event as a counter narrative to the complete defeat of the native peoples. According to the Nahuatl-language *Nican Mopohua* apparitions narrative (a title derived from the document's first words, "here is recounted"), which devotees acclaim as the foundational text of the Guadalupe tradition, her first words to the indigenous neophyte Juan Diego (whom Pope John Paul II canonized a saint in 2002) are "dignified Juan, dignified Juan Diego." She then goes on to give him the mission of communicating to Juan de Zumárraga, the first bishop of Mexico, her desire that a temple be built on the hill of Tepeyac where she "will show and give to all people all my love, my compassion, my help, and my protection."[17] Juan Diego's joyful confidence soon dissipates, as he is made to wait an extended time before he is permitted to see the bishop, who clearly appears incredulous at the *indio*'s testimony. After a series of further encounters with Guadalupe and interviews with the bishop, the story reaches its climax: the doubting bishop comes to believe when Juan Diego drops exquisite out-of-season flowers from his *tilma* (cloak) and presents the image of Guadalupe that miraculously appeared on the rough cloth of his garment. In various ways Guadalupe provided Juan Diego with hope and consolation, especially through the healing of his uncle, Juan Bernardino.

Guadalupe's words of comfort and calling are given effect in the narrative's dramatic reversals. At the beginning of the story only Guadalupe has trust in Juan Diego; by the end the bishop and his assistants believe he is truly her messenger. At the outset of the account Juan Diego comes meekly before the bishop; in the end the stooped *indio* stands erect while the bishop and his household kneel before him and venerate the image on his *tilma*. Throughout the account Juan Diego must journey to the center of the city from Tepeyac some three miles to the north; at the end of the narration the bishop and his entourage accompany Juan Diego to Tepeyac, where they will build the temple that Our Lady of Guadalupe requested. Symbolically, the presence of the ecclesial leadership and the church they are constructing are thus moved from the center of their capital out to the margins among the indigenous people. The transformations realized through Guadalupe initiate a process of reconciliation and justice, the breaking in of God's reign that upends the status quo of the world. Virgilio deems Guadalupe "the compassionate mother of the new people, who will build a new temple, the dynamic, living force which will bring about self-esteem, liberation, and peace."[18]

The evangelical vision mediated in the Guadalupe account is not solely a call to comfort, but "a dynamic call to action." As Virgilio concludes, in events like the Guadalupe encounter God "gives to those poor who put their trust in Him a new vision of themselves — from being nothing and despised [like Juan Diego] to being children of the Almighty — so that together they might initiate the process of liberty and life for everyone." Confronting the violence of the conquest, Guadalupe initiates a "new order [that] would not be European and it would not be a simple continuation of the previous one, but as the flower comes from the seed, so their new life would now arise from the old."[19] The Guadalupe apparition narrative engenders hope that the drama of Juan Diego and Juan de Zumárraga reveals a divine plan in which the humanity and dignity of the lowly are restored, injustice is set aright, strangers become friends, enemies are reconciled, and the love of a common mother incites mutual respect and harmony. But it is also an urgent plea that the final resolution of this drama has yet to be realized in individual lives, families, communities, the church, and society. Our enduring task as disciples is to enact this Gospel vision proclaimed in Guadalupe. Celebrations in her honor rejuvenate this vision among her growing body of faithful both annually on her feast day and in the daily devotions of her daughters and sons.

Virgilio's subsequent writings deepened these initial analyses and further extended his spiritual reflections on Guadalupe. The several excerpts from his writings on Guadalupe in chapter 3 of this anthology illustrate his rich reflections, illuminating insights about Christian life such as the gratuitousness of divine love, the *imago dei,* the power of communal faith celebrations, evangelization, and conversion. He expanded on Guadalupe's role among the conquered indigenous in Mexico to explore the ways she has enabled Mexican Americans to maintain their dignity in the long wake of the U.S. conquest of northern Mexico.

Guadalupe, whom he describes as a *mestiza,* "the first truly American person and as such the mother of the new generations to come,"[20] provides hope and inspiration for Mexican Americans struggling to embrace their identity as *mestizos,* synthesize the richness from their parent cultures, and lead the way in constructing a society in which the barriers between peoples are broken. For Christians of any background, Our Lady of Guadalupe announces the Gospel message that discipleship requires listening to the voice of the forgotten and marginalized, defending and helping them to sense their dignity as God's sons and daughters, and preferentially choosing them as the recipients of the church's proclamation of the Gospel, service, and struggle for a more just social order.

Theology as Spiritual Discernment

Born of life experience and pastoral practice, Virgilio Elizondo's theology is more than just critical thinking about faith. For Virgilio, theology is a spiritual discernment that examines the human situation, judges it in light of the Gospels, acts to transform whatever obscures our innate beauty as creatures made in God's image, and celebrates the transformations that have already dawned in Christ. His writings offer a clear and concrete articulation of goodness and beauty in everyday life, as well as of sin and its effects. He also presents a divine plan that illuminates a truth larger than the visible realities of present struggles and suffering and gives people a reason for hope. This Gospel vision summons his listeners to discipleship: a commitment both to prayer and the action that flows from it and leads back to it.

The organizational structure of this book mirrors the see-judge-act-celebrate approach that marks Virgilio's writings as spiritual discernment. Chapter 1 presents an overview of the life journey from which his spiritual writings emerged, illuminating his analyses of his human situation and that of his Mexican American people, as well as the contours of personal experience that shape his perceptions. The middle two chapters explore God's response to our longings as revealed in the Gospel witness of Jesus and in Our Lady of Guadalupe as a proclamation of the Gospel in the Americas. Chapter 4 concludes the anthology with meditations on following Christ in the joy, celebration, and evangelical living of discipleship. Each chapter encompasses reflections on Virgilio's core insights about the centrality of *mestizaje* to Mexican American experience and to a deeper understanding of Jesus, Mary of Guadalupe, and the call to discipleship. Virgilio's recurrent emphasis on Mexican American celebrations and faith expressions as a window into their collective spirit is also illuminated in excerpts from his writings interspersed throughout the volume. The criteria for choosing selections were to represent the range of Virgilio's insights on all these central topics in his thought and to probe the life and faith experiences that gave birth to his reflections. Excerpts from his major publications complement selections from his shorter essays, homilies, and other lesser known works.

Above all else, Virgilio is a pastor who perceives in his people's daily struggles the universal human quest for a sense of worth and belonging. God's response to these longings is Jesus of Galilee and his mother whom Mexican Americans know as Our Lady of Guadalupe. The Galilean Jesus and Guadalupe enable us to confront the self-doubt and low self-esteem that damage our faith in the God who made us in the divine image. They lead us to counter the sinful in-group/out-group dynamics that plague fallen humanity. They give us hope of the new life that unites the world's diverse peoples at the banquet table of God. Virgilio's writings are a spiritual breakthrough in that they present a graced instance where the life experience of a Christian disciple and his faith community meet and retell the Gospel story. Welcome to this anthology, which reveals the spirituality at the core of Virgilio's life, pastoral leadership, and theological vision.

Notes

1. Virgilio Elizondo, *A God of Incredible Surprises: Jesus of Galilee* (Lanham, Md.: Rowman and Littlefield, 2003), 1.

2. Virgilio Elizondo, presentation to the Continental Conference of African Theologians (typescript), Harare, Zimbabwe, January 18, 1991.

3. Virgilio Elizondo, *A Search for Meaning in Life and Death* (Manila, Philippines: East Asian Pastoral Institute, 1971); reprinted as *The Human Quest: A Search for Meaning through Life and Death* (Huntington, Ind.: Our Sunday Visitor, 1978), 13.

4. Ibid., 17.

5. Ibid., 32.

6. Ibid., especially chapter 2, "Genesis." Teilhard de Chardin completed *The Phenomenon of Man* in the 1930s. It was first published posthumously in 1955 and has been released in various subsequent printings, including the 1965 release that Virgilio cites extensively (New York: Harper and Row) in *The Human Quest.* For a further treatment of Teilhard de Chardin's influence on Virgilio, see Alejandro García-Rivera, "Crossing Theological Borders: Virgilio Elizondo's Place among Theologians of Culture," in *Beyond Borders: Writings of Virgilio Elizondo and Friends,* ed. Timothy Matovina (Maryknoll, N.Y.: Orbis Books, 2000), 246–56; Eduardo González Oropeza, *Mestizaje e Intellectus Fidei: Acercamiento Teológico Fundamental* (Rome: Pontificiae Universitatis Gregorianae, 2007), especially 18–19, 23–37.

7. Elizondo, *Human Quest,* 77.

8. Ibid., 80–81.

9. Ibid., 144.

10. John A. Coleman, "Virgilio Elizondo: Practical Theologian, Prophet, and Organic Intellectual," in *Beyond Borders,* 243.

11. Jacques Audinet, "Preface," in Virgilio Elizondo, *Galilean Journey: The Mexican-American Promise* (Maryknoll, N.Y.: Orbis Books, 1983), xi. Entitled *Métissage, violence culturelle, annonce de l'Evangile,* Virgilio's dissertation was published as *Mestizaje: The Dialectic of Cultural Birth and the Gospel,* 3 vols. (San Antonio: Mexican American Cultural Center Press, 1978).

12. Elizondo, *Galilean Journey,* 1.

13. Ibid., 47.

14. Ibid., 72.

15. Ibid., 125.

16. Virgilio Elizondo, *La Morenita: Evangelizer of the Americas* (San Antonio: Mexican American Cultural Center Press, 1980), 50.

17. Citations from the *Nican Mopohua* are taken from the translation provided in Virgilio Elizondo, *Guadalupe: Mother of the New Creation* (Maryknoll, N.Y.: Orbis Books, 1997), 7, 8.

18. Elizondo, *La Morenita*, 90.

19. Ibid., 90, 95, 98.

20. Elizondo, *La Morenita*, 112; Virgilio Elizondo, *The Future Is Mestizo: Life Where Cultures Meet*, rev. ed. (Boulder: University Press of Colorado, 2000), 65.

1

Life Journey

Along with many of my people, I too was searching for answers. — *The Future Is Mestizo*, 67

Spiritual writing is intrinsically autobiographical. Our ultimate questions — about the suffering of the innocent, the wellsprings of human compassion, the numinous experience of falling in love, the wonders of creation, the mystery of death, the afterlife, the meaning and purpose of life itself — are deeply rooted in personal and collective histories. The writings of Virgilio Elizondo are no exception. As the selections in this chapter reveal, his formative experiences in a loving family and community were the initial source for many of his spiritual insights. His Mexican American people's struggles for dignity have consistently shaped his outlook and spiritual writings. The Mexican Catholic rituals and devotions practiced and cherished in his home parish were a source of ridicule among his seminary classmates and professors, but he endeavored to examine those practices more deeply and revive them in his ministry as a priest. Mestizaje, living between cultures, has been a daily reality from his early years to the present and is a central theme in his thought.

The selections in this chapter narrate Virgilio's reflections on his life journey. They are taken from a variety of sources, several of them from his book The Future Is Mestizo, *itself a work of autobiography with final chapters of theological reflection on Guadalupe, the Galilean Jesus, and* mestizaje *as a pathway forward for divided humanity. As chapters 2 and 3 of this anthology will further illuminate, the thread that unites the tapestry of his life is the search for the interrelations between his own experiences, the struggles and joys of his Mexican American people, and the Gospel stories of Jesus, along with the corresponding image and apparition account of Our Lady of Guadalupe. Virgilio's spirituality closely parallels the title of his major book,* Galilean Journey. *Read together, the following selections reveal the unfolding of a life that found its deepest fulfillment in the recognition that Jesus of Galilee is the key to understanding, celebrating, and transforming our lives, in Virgilio's particular case the life of* mestizos *in the U.S.–Mexico borderlands.*

FAMILY AND NEIGHBORHOOD

Virgilio Elizondo was born in San Antonio on August 26, 1935, the second of two children born to Virgilio and Ana María (née Peimbert) Elizondo. His formative experiences in family, neighborhood, and parish provided an enduring spiritual foundation for later struggles, but especially for Virgilio's characteristic joy in good times and in bad. The starting point for his spiritual journey is the communal experience of family, faith, and fiesta, which he narrates vividly in the following passage.

My parents owned and operated a small grocery store, which was not only a family business but also, along with the local Catholic church, the center of community life and exchange of news. The women would take their time doing the shopping, while the men waited in the backyard drinking beer, exchanging "men stories," and telling good jokes. Everyone knew each other by name and had a sincere interest in the needs and goings-on of people in the neighborhood. Many of the customers not only bought from us, but would help with the cleaning up and other aspects of the business. If my father wanted to go fishing, he would simply close the store and go. If the fish were biting, he would bring back plenty to give away to everyone. If he didn't catch any, we would have a lot of good stories to tell about the ones that got away. The store was hard work, but it was fun.

We had a small home, which was shared by my parents, my sister and me, my mother's mother (Doña María Manuela Petra Paula Ester Fernández del Castillo viuda de Peimbert), my father's father (Don Antonio), three canaries, two cats, and two beautiful German police dogs named Kaiser and Tarzan. It was a simple home — no hot water, a wood stove, and an old icebox. Today it would be unthinkable. Yet in those days, we were not aware that we were missing anything. Besides, my grandmother was an accomplished cook and not only did we never lack for a good meal, but there was always extra food for an unexpected visitor.

Looking back, I can see that we were not rich or even middle class, but we never lacked anything, especially a lot of personal care and affection. If my mother got after us for something, my grandmother was always around to console us and spoil us. There were always neighborhood kids around and the whole neighborhood was one big extended family. Materially we did not have much, but socially we were most fortunate. We never looked upon ourselves as deprived of anything. In fact, I think we were truly of a privileged class — one in which tender, loving concern was the ordinary rule of the day and in which hard work was intermingled with many good times.

My parents were both immigrants from Mexico. My father had come from a very large and very poor family in the small town of Rosales in northern Mexico. At the age of thirteen, he had been sent to San Antonio to seek out an uncle who had a grocery store so that he could work there and send some money home. In those days there were no trains or buses in that region of the country. My dad did not know any English whatsoever and he was walking into totally unknown lands. He walked and asked for rides and gradually traveled the more than two hundred miles of near desert lands under the blistering sun of Texas. Even that he arrived is a small miracle in itself. Similar stories continue today as thousands of poor people struggle to escape the disastrous conditions of Mexico and Central America.

My father never had much schooling, but he was gifted with wisdom and practical knowhow. He never went beyond the third grade, yet I have never met a more educated man. He had a gift for sizing up the situation and making a quick practical conclusion. He could add numbers just by looking at them much quicker than someone else could with an adding machine.

He endured many hardships — long working hours, poor living conditions, harsh treatment because he was a working nephew and not one of the sons of the family. Yet the hardships did not embitter him or dampen his enthusiasm. Life was never easy for him, but he did not allow the struggles for life and survival to dominate him; rather he dominated and conquered them. His constant sense of humor and his great generosity toward those in need are still legendary among those who knew him. He was a very good businessman and could have become rich quite easily if he had wanted to, but instead he chose to love life and live it to the fullest.

My mother came from a totally different setting. She had been born of a very wealthy family in Mexico City. Their family home was a thirty-six room mansion in the most fashionable section of Mexico City. My great grandfather had emigrated from France, and my grandfather had been a very successful engineer in Mexico City. The family had enjoyed the life of leisure of high-society Mexico until all tumbled to a quick end with the unexpected death of my grandfather. Those were not the days of insurance policies, and my grandmother knew absolutely nothing about her husband's business.

Those were also the days of great political turmoil in Mexico. Governments were changing every few days and were consistently troubled by the revolutionaries who were passing through. My grandmother was a young widow with two beautiful young daughters living in a huge mansion in Mexico City. She had no money to support herself although the home gave the appearance of great wealth. They had dropped from wealth to poverty overnight. Luckily, her older sister had married a *norte-americano* — a man from the United States — who was willing to bring my mother and grandmother with him to the United States. They were fortunate, yet it was still difficult. An incredible and unimagined new life of hardships and joys awaited them in the new land of opportunity.

Working was so much below the dignity of the high-class ladies of Mexico, but there was no choice. So my grandmother started to work and my mother continued her education in a Catholic college for young women. My mother never forgot when one of the nuns asked her to give her class work to one of the wealthy girls in the class because the wealthy girl's parents would never understand her low grade! Those who had little or nothing were to give what little they had to those who already had too much. That seems to be the unwritten law of so many civilizations: the poor work hard to make it easy for the rich to reap and enjoy the rewards of the efforts of the unfortunate.

My mother quickly got a job as a secretary, but it wasn't easy to go from a carefree existence in Mexico to the demanding life of a legal secretary in the United States. My mother has always expressed gratitude for the patience of the first Anglo lawyers who hired her and patiently worked with her as she struggled with legal terminology in a language she was just beginning to learn. Yet she had the determination to succeed and she became an excellent secretary.

My parents met at a Tuesday Night Dance Club, and after a few years they decided to get married. All their friends thought they were crazy. Those were the Depression years. They didn't have any property, any money, and apparently any future. Yet love has reasons that reason will never be able to reason to. So they started. It was the union of two very unlikely persons — for my mother and father were totally different. Yet as far as I can remember, they made a perfect match. I have never known a more loving and more caring couple. One of my greatest treasures is the memory of this love and concern of my parents for one another and together for their family. In them, I saw and experienced the unlimited love of God.

My father never learned English well, but that was never an obstacle to his ability to communicate effectively in either English or Spanish. He developed a good business and the respect of everyone. He would easily walk right past the secretaries into the manager's office of any of the places we did business with and was proud of his good credit rating at the Frost Bank, San Antonio's leading bank. In time, he helped to start the first bank owned by Latinos: the West Side State Bank — "West Side" having a pejorative connotation in San Antonio since it is the district in which the poorest Mexicans live.

If he had inferiority complexes or painful memories about his past, I was not aware of them. He was a hard worker, a deeply religious man (though not churchy), and very dedicated to the betterment of *nuestra mexicanidad* within the United States. He loved the United States because of the liberty and free spirit that reigned here. Yet he would get very upset at the gross stereotypes that the people of the United States had about Mexicans. He became a proud and loyal citizen of the U.S.A., but this did not mean he wanted to cease being who he was. Our Mexican background and language were always regarded as a treasured honor — never to be forgotten for the sake of our new civic identity.

My mother always had the ability to be a good listener. Doña Anita not only helped run the store but she helped people in the organizing and running of their lives. It seems that there were always school kids from the neighborhood visiting with her. She would spend time with kids from broken homes, encourage school dropouts to return to school, tell young girls how to be proper *señoritas,* and build a sense of self-pride in all the kids who visited her. Many of the salesmen would come by more to visit with her than to get orders. She was the neighborhood psychologist. Many of the professionals around San Antonio today remember that it was she who consistently made them feel good about themselves and encouraged them to keep working hard at school to succeed. It is amazing how many people around San Antonio had good wisdom to share because of what they received from her.

My sister, like myself, always brought many friends around the house. Our home served as the community recreation center, for our friends were always around. I don't remember ever getting bored or lonely. When we were not working in the store, we were playing in one way or another. We had great childhood games that served as a natural initiation into the whole process of life.

I always admired my sister very much, although I hated the fact that she didn't have to study to make good grades while I had to slave through the books merely to make a passing grade. In the early years, studies always appeared so boring. She has talents that I would love to have, but don't. She is an excellent artist and musician. Today her works of art can be found on exhibit around the country.

My early home memories would not be complete without a mention of my grandmother. Her life and example have been one of the deep and lasting influences on my life. She lived a simple existence, like what you would expect of a pious monk. She had a very simple room and never dressed in fancy clothing. I don't remember ever seeing any jewelry on her. Her time was spent in prayer, visiting from her window with anyone who passed by, or in the kitchen fixing the noonday meal. The odors that came from the kitchen still make my mouth water today. She was a true artist of the kitchen.

But what I remember the most was her philosophy of life. She was one of the happiest women I have ever met. She radiated inner peace, serenity, and happiness. She used to say that the greatest gift God had given to her was having taken everything away from her. In my younger years, this did not make any sense, since I always wanted to have more things. Yet in time, it made more and more sense to me. In Mexico, she had had great material comforts. Yet in losing material wealth, she started to discover deeper things in life. In the simple but joy-filled existence of our home-store in San Antonio, she had discovered the true things that were worth living for. She had, in effect, discovered the mystery of life.

For all practical purposes, our neighborhood could have been a small town in Mexico. Everyone spoke Spanish. The occasional English-speaking person passing through the neighborhood always seemed to be an oddity. We were all Catholics and the few Protestants around seemed to be from another planet.

The only institution in the area that was clearly Anglo-Saxon-Protestant-U.S.A. was the public school, where all the teachers were from another part of town and of course non-Spanish-speaking. The school grounds were like a little island of the U.S.A. within Mexico. There the kids were forbidden to speak Spanish and even punished for doing so. While at home we heard about the Alamo traitors, at school they were presented as the Alamo heroes.* Much later on in life, I was to learn that there are various versions of history — all true, but no one of them exhaustive. The ones that appear as traitors to one are the heroes of the other. The freedom fighters of one side are the terrorists of the other.

But in my own first experiences of school, I was very fortunate. My parents sent me to the parish kindergarten operated by Mexican nuns, the Cordi Marian Sisters. It was simply an extension of the home. The sisters did their shopping in our grocery store as did the parish priests. They frequently visited our home, and all the families from the area felt welcome in the convent and kindergarten. We not only had school, but dances, plays, games, and all kinds of activities. We had a wonderful experience of belonging.

---

*The Alamo was the site of the famous 1836 battle in which the Mexican army of General Antonio López de Santa Anna defeated forces fighting for Texas under the command of Colonel William Barret Travis.

The local parish was always full of activity. Sunday Mass was but one of the many activities that attracted us to the parish. Before the days of television, the parish had weekly movies — cowboys and Indians, detective, romance. Sometimes they were in Spanish and other times in English, but they were always great fun. The many novenas, processions, crownings, and special devotions kept us all entertained. Church was the best circus anywhere. We loved it. The church was the center of life. It was the community living room where we all met and enjoyed each other. From birth and baptism to the last anointing and funeral it permeated our lives and gave us the experience of being a united family. — *The Future Is Mestizo*, 4–11

LOVE GIVES LIFE

Though his father died when Virgilio was in his late twenties and his mother in 2001, he recounts memories of them and extended family members in his writings, homilies, and presentations. The following selection reveals the enduring influence his parents' life of charity has had on him and others from his neighborhood.

At my mother's funeral, a former employee of our family's grocery store came and told me how much my parents meant to him and how much they had done for him. The young man remembered an act of kindness by our dad that changed his whole life. When he was a young boy in elementary school, he was the butt of everyone's cruel jokes because he was tall for his age and mentally slow. One day on his way to school he saw my father sweeping the sidewalk in front of the store and stopped to talk to him. My father complained that because there was a bus stop in front of the store, there was always a lot of trash and no one bothered to sweep it up. The next morning, this young boy got up very early, took his mother's broom, and went and swept the sidewalk in front of the store before my father opened the store. He continued to do this for several days until one early morning he found my father waiting for him. My father told him he was so pleased with the job the young man was doing that he wanted to hire him to continue doing it and pay him.

When the young man went to school that day and told everyone that Mr. Elizondo had just hired him to work at the store, everyone was in awe. No other child in the school had a paying job. That afternoon several of his classmates came by the store to see if it was true and if they could get a job too, but my father told them that he had hired the young man because he did such a fine job and he could depend on him. After this, he said, "No one teased me anymore. They all respected me because Mr. Elizondo had given me a paying job." The recognition of his talent had transformed his shame into pride; in many ways, it had given him life....

My dad ran the store, but my mom was the neighborhood counselor. It is amazing to me today how often I run into very successful persons who tell me that it was thanks to my mother's encouragement and advice that they decided to stay in school and go to college. In the days I was growing up in San Antonio, many of our public schools discouraged Mexican American youth from advancing in education. They often convinced our children that they were not good enough to even think about the professions. My mother countered this by constantly bringing out the good and challenging them to believe in themselves and go for the top. I have come to learn that this is a profound aspect of charity: not just helping people in material need, but also helping the needy to believe in themselves, to appreciate their dignity, to value their infinite worth, and to dare to achieve what society and its teachers tell them they are incapable of obtaining. Mom was a master at this. This is the deepest root of my preaching and teaching today, for it really pains me to see how many people do not believe in themselves or value their talents and abilities and hence waste their lives away feeling sorry for themselves. At my mother's funeral a childhood friend came up to my sister and me and said: "Memi [as her friends used to call her] was our Mother Teresa."

My parents knew that just helping others in need was not enough. We had to help change the society that made life miserable for our people and excluded us from many of the structures of opportunity. My parents and most of the people in our neighborhood became citizens so that they could vote and take part in the decision-making process. This was a great country but far from perfect, and the exciting thing was that we could take a part in making it better. I remember the great enthusiasm as I went with my dad to meetings of associations for the betterment of our people. Even if it was difficult, we had to work to break down the walls of exclusion that kept so many people in misery. From my earliest days, I remember our involvement in civic and cultural causes. I remember selling bingo tickets to help elect Henry González as our first Mexican American city councilman. He eventually became our first U.S. congressman and one of the most respected members of Congress. Today, his son Charlie González has succeeded him at this post. We worked hard to help repeal the poll tax that had been designed to keep poor blacks and Mexican Americans from voting. Civic involvement was collective charity in action.

—*Charity*, 121–22, 27–29

LA MARAVILLA

Many of Virgilio's later reflections are rooted in his memorable experiences as a child and young adult, such as the following passage that links recollections of festive gatherings at his family farm with the table fellowship of Jesus.

In my father's grocery store in the Mexican neighborhood of San Antonio, the biggest vegetables, the tastiest fruit, the most tender meats, and the best chickens and turkeys were always said to come from my father's ranch and farm, which, because of its many marvels, was known as La Maravilla. Even the finest milk, butter, and cheeses were said to come from the wonderful cows and goats of La Maravilla. From its reputation, one would certainly get the impression that La Maravilla was a huge estate of thousands of acres of the finest grazing lands and the most fertile fields.

Actually, it was only a two-acre piece of land on the outskirts of San Antonio along the banks of the Medina River with nothing more than a few jack rabbits, squirrels, and snakes moving between the cacti, mesquite trees, and other wild shrubs. What gave rise to the very popular myth of the great marvels of La Maravilla was not the physical things it produced but the marvelous fellowship that was experienced there.

Every Sunday, *mi papá* would take a carload of *chorizos,* meats, and chickens to barbecue. There would be plenty of salads, beans, corn on the cob, lemonade, and beer for anyone who wanted to come. My college friends of all ethnic, religious, and social backgrounds would come just as easily as friends from the neighborhood and professional people who were friends of *Papá*. Without any concern for anyone's background or identity, the friendly conversation could easily go from world affairs to neighborhood gossip, to joke telling to anything else. No topic was out of place, and no one ever felt out of place. Whoever came was equally welcomed, and there was always plenty of food and drink for everyone. At La Maravilla we were all friends and cared about each other. People came not because they already cared about each other, but in the midst of the fellowship produced by the food and drink they shared in common, they became friends and started to care for one another. This was the community of La Maravilla, whose marvels became known as a paradise on earth full of the best things of the earth. In actuality it had only the very best: a community of friends where everyone who came experienced unconditional welcome; a place where strangers became friends and friends rejoiced in the company of one another.

My dad has been dead for more than thirty years, yet for those who remember, the myth of La Maravilla continues to grow and enliven our lives. I suppose that this is where I first experienced the creative force and life-giving joy of table fellowship. The weekly feasts at La Maravilla did not seem like anything religious any more than the table parties of Jesus appeared to be a religious celebration. In hindsight I realize, through reflections on the way of Jesus, that I was taking part in the purest of any religious ritual: the joy of inclusive table fellowship and a foretaste of the eternal banquet in heaven at the end of time.   — *A God of Incredible Surprises*, 87–88

CROSSING BORDERS

A common quip among Mexican Americans in San Antonio is that their hometown is "the northernmost city in Mexico." It is certainly a place where Mexico meets the United States. The daily reality of living between cultural worlds — even in his own hometown — was formative for Virgilio as it has been for many others. In particular, Virgilio's jarring experience of otherness in his grade school and discomfort when he visited Mexico exemplifies the borderland existence of Mexican Americans, a reality that comprises both the context and a consistent theme in his spiritual writings.

During my boyhood days there were no questions whatsoever about my identity or belonging. We grew up at home wherever we went — playgrounds, school, church. The whole atmosphere was Mexican and there were no doubts in our minds about the pride of being Mexican. Radio stations provided us with good Mexican music, and the local Mexican theaters kept us in contact with the dances, folklore, romance, and daily life of Mexico. The poverty of Mexico, which was always evident in the movies, was completely surpassed by the natural simplicity, ingenuity, graciousness, and joy of the Mexican people. The

United States was so efficient, but Mexico was so human. The contrasts were clear. We might be living outside the political boundaries of Mexico, but Mexico was not outside of us. We continued to interiorize it with great pride.

Como México no hay dos — there is nothing else like Mexico. Being Mexican was the greatest gift of God's grace. We loved it, lived it, and celebrated it. In many ways, we felt sorry for the people who were not so lucky as to be Mexican. In those early years I never thought of myself as a native-born U.S. citizen of Mexican descent. My U.S. identity was quite secondary to my Mexican identity. Yet I was happy living in the United States. We belonged to this land called the United States and this land belonged to us. In those early days, I never experienced being Mexican as not belonging. This was my home. I was born here and I belonged here.

Little did I think in those early years that the foundations of a new identity were already being formed within me. I was living a new identity that had not yet been defined and that would take many years to emerge. The new identity was beginning to emerge, not as a theory of evolution or as a political ideology of one type or another. It was rather a life lived not just by me, but by thousands of others who were living a similar experience. We were the first of a new human group that was beginning to emerge.

The paradise existence of the neighborhood came to a halt the first day I went to a Catholic grade school operated by German nuns in what had been a German parish. There the pastor still told Mexicans to go away because it wasn't their church. My parents had sent me there because it was the nearest Catholic school. Mexicans were tolerated but not very welcome.

The next few years would be a real purgatory. The new language was completely foreign to me and everything was strange. The food in the cafeteria was horrible — sauerkraut and other foods that I only remember as weird. We were not allowed to speak Spanish and were punished when we got caught doing so.

The sisters and lay teachers were strict disciplinarians. I don't think I ever saw them smile, but I remember well them hitting us frequently with a ruler or a stick. They were the exact opposite of the Mexican sisters around our home who were always happy, joking, and smiling and formed us carefully through counsels, suggestions, and rewards. In one system we were punished for bad things we did while in the other we were rewarded for our good accomplishments.

Mass was so different. Everything was orderly and stern. People seemed to be in pain and even afraid of being there. It was a church of discipline, but it was not one of joy. In fact, joy seemed to be out of place. Mass was recited, not celebrated. People went because they had to, not because they wanted to. It seemed like a totally different religion.

It was hard going to school in a language that was almost completely unknown and in surroundings that were so foreign and alienating. Things did not make sense. I used to get very bored. The school hours seemed eternal; the clock appeared not even to move during those horribly unintelligible hours. My parents had to force me to study, and it was very difficult for me even to make passing grades. Going to school was so different that it was like crossing the border every day, like going to another country to go to school, even though it was only a few blocks from our home.

It was during these days that I first started to get a feeling of being a foreigner in the very country in which I had been born and raised. Guilt started to develop within me: Why wasn't I like the other children who spoke English and ate sandwiches rather than *tortillas?* I started to feel different and mixed up about who I was. But the mixture and the bad feelings came to a quick end every day at three o'clock when school was dismissed and I returned home. It was the beginning of life in two countries that were worlds apart.

I wanted to become what I felt I had to be, for it was my parents, whose authority and wisdom I never questioned, who had sent me to that school. Yet it meant not so much developing myself as ceasing to be who I was in order to become another person. Those three years in primary school were awful. I was afraid to mix with the kids and often felt better going off by myself. The teachers were constantly getting after me for day-dreaming. That was my natural escape mechanism or, better yet, my instinct to survive. The dreams were my spontaneous efforts to create an existence of my own, thus refusing to accept the existence that was being imposed upon me.

As I look into the past and try to understand it from my present perspective many years later, I reexperience the original pain, sadness, embarrassment, ambiguity, frustration, and the sense of seeking refuge by being alone. Yet I can also see that it was already the beginning of the formation of the consciousness of a new existence — of a new *mestizaje* (the process through which two totally different peoples mix biologically and culturally so that a new people begins to emerge). The daily border crossing was having its effect on me. I didn't know what it meant. I didn't even know why it had to be. But that constant crossing became the most ordinary thing in my life. In spite of the contradictions at school, there was never any serious doubt in my mind that my original home experience in a Mexican neighborhood was the core of my existence and identity; there my belonging was never questioned. There I did not seek to go off by myself but was developing into quite an outgoing person.

By the time I was ten, my parents moved me to another school in downtown San Antonio. It was the old German school called St. Joseph's. There things started to change for me. I ended up with a teacher who was a German-American from an Alsatian congregation — Sister Michael Rose. She was one that combined demanding discipline with lots of love and understanding. She always had the most beautiful smile and even when she had to correct us she did it in such a way that she never put us down. She was stern but friendly; she was interested in our family life and took a personal interest in each one of her students. For the first time, a teacher of another nationality was not a distant other. She was a friend. That made all the difference.

All of a sudden, school started to be exciting. I actually stayed after school hours to help the teacher and do extra work. The old contradiction between home and school was not present — or maybe I had simply gotten used to it and had started to assimilate it. I made new friends of various ethnic backgrounds and enjoyed running around with them after school hours.

But walking around the downtown area every day brought some new experiences. I started to discover blacks. Before, I had never even known about their existence. Those were still the days of segregation when the blacks had to sit in special "colored balconies" in the theaters, attend black churches, sit in the back of the public buses, and use separate toilets in public places. Many of my school friends had darker skin than myself, and I remember well the problems we experienced just trying to go to the toilet. If we went into the one marked "colored" we were chased out by the blacks because we were not technically black. Yet we were often chased out from the ones marked "white" because we had dark skin. So we didn't even have toilets to which we could go. Our being was actually our "nonbeing." This consciousness of "nonbeing" would deepen and broaden as I gradually moved from a very secure experience of being, to one of nonbeing, to one of new being.

The schools had done a good job of convincing us that we were different, but the schools were trying to help us be ordinary and like everyone else. They did not say we were different or inferior in so many words, but they did not have to. All the courses indicated this by pointing to the Anglo-American models of existence as the only normal existence of intelligent, civilized human beings. How could we want to be otherwise? To be otherwise was backward, underdeveloped, somewhat stupid — that is, inferior.

During these early years, I realized more and more that I could easily adjust to the Anglo-American ways of the U.S.A., yet there was never any doubt that my family was *puro mexicano*. We prided ourselves on everything Mexican. One of the most fascinating days in the life of the entire neighborhood was when the Mexican soccer team came to play in San Antonio and defeated the U.S. team. It was as if Mexico had conquered the U.S.A. We were jubilant with joy and pride.

We did not attempt to define what it meant to be Mexican. We did not have to. We knew who we were and we were proud and happy to be just that. With equal degrees of certitude we knew we were not Spaniards, we knew we were not Indians, and we knew we were Mexican. We did not go into our origins but simply loved and celebrated our existential identity. If the U.S. was the land of opportunity and development, Mexico was the land of ancient civilizations, sophisticated culture, and beautiful customs and traditions. The U.S. had a great future; Mexico had a great past....

Yet this certitude of being Mexican began to be questioned whenever we visited our relatives in Mexico. Even though they loved us and we loved to visit them, in many ways they would let us know that we were *pochos* — Mexicans from the United States. To this day, it is not uncommon to hear someone in Mexico say about a Mexican American's Spanish, "For a *norteamericano,* your Spanish is not so bad." Yet it is not uncommon for an Anglo-American from the United States to say about a Mexican American speaking perfect English, "For a Mexican American your English is pretty good." Whether in Mexico or the United States we are always the distant and different "other." The core of our existence is to be "other" or to "not be" in relation to those who are. Yet being called *pocho* in Mexico was not insulting, for we were fully accepted. There was always rejoicing when our families visited us in San Antonio or when we visited them in Mexico. *Pocho* was simply a reality. Even though the United States was our home, it was in Mexico that we felt more and more at home. The label marked distance and difference but not separation or rejection.

This was an experience totally different from being called "Meskins," "Greasers," or "wetbacks" in the United States. The titles were used to remind us that we were different — meaning that we were backward, ignorant, inferior, scum. We were not wanted in the United States, merely tolerated and exploited. Our people were consistently subjected to multiple injustices. The movies depicted us as treacherous bandits or drunken fools and our women as wanting nothing better in life than to go to bed with one of the white masters. Anglo-American society had no doubts that it alone was the Master Race!   — *The Future Is Mestizo*, 12–21

VOCATION

While pursuing his undergraduate studies at San Antonio's St. Mary's University, where he earned a bachelor degree in chemistry in 1957, Virgilio discerned a call to serve as a priest.

I had decided to study chemistry and social sciences because I was interested in working with people by becoming either a medical doctor or a psychiatrist. Yet as university studies proceeded I became more convinced that the best way to work with people — especially my own people, many of whom were poor, uneducated, and unemployed — would be through the church. The archbishop of San Antonio, Robert E. Lucey, was an untiring champion of the rights of the poor and of the need to work for a just society. He consistently brought to light the many injustices that condemned Mexicans and blacks to a life of perpetual poverty and misery. People disliked him because he stood up for the oppressed and marginalized of society, because he dared to proclaim what others tried to hide and ignore.

I realized that I was one of the fortunate ones. God had given me the opportunity for a good education. Yet the masses of my people did not have such opportunities. I started to struggle with the sense of an obligation to dedicate my life to the betterment of my people. More and more, I found myself dropping by chapel to be alone with God to discern what I should do with myself. I never spoke to anyone about this except God, and the final decision was between God and myself. By the time I started to seek information on how to become a priest, I already knew that I would be one.   — *The Future Is Mestizo*, 23–24

SEMINARY STRUGGLES

During Virgilio's seminary formation the friendships he developed with others at the seminary, the support of the Carmelite priests in his home parish, and summer months spent among family and friends sustained him. But as one of just a handful of Mexican American seminarians, he often found his theological education and formation distanced him from his people, their heritage, and their faith expressions. Only later did he perceive more fully the implications of this process of alienation, especially through reflection on experiences such as the following incident.

In the early 1970s, we were having a vocation conference at the Mexican American Cultural Center. There were several bishops, priests, religious, and many Mexican American laity. All kinds of suggestions were made as to how we could recruit more Mexican Americans into the priesthood and religious life. One couple came up to the podium and told us why they hoped and prayed that none of their sons or daughters would ever become religious or priests. They stated: "We don't want to lose them from the family." Everyone was stunned! They were against the very purpose for which we had all gathered. I immediately reacted (as I am sure many others did) by thinking that we too had to be generous and let go of our children so that they could become priests or religious. But before I could respond, they had already started to explain themselves:

> If one of our sons or daughters became a religious or priest, and the Church sent them to Africa, China, or some other distant place, and we never saw them again in our lives, that would not be losing them from the family. In fact, we would be gaining the people they worked with into our family and we would be honored and proud.
>
> What we mean by losing them from the family is that when one of our daughters or sons goes to the convent or seminary, they come home to visit us ashamed of who we are, especially of how we pray and how we express and practice our faith. This is losing them from the family!

There was a profound silence in the room. No one dared to respond; no one at that moment had an answer. These simple and unassuming barrio parents had pronounced a prophetic word which was immediately evident. They had identified the root of the problem: U.S. Catholicism was ashamed of our Mexican Catholicism, and thus to become good priests or religious in the United States, we had to assume that shame of our own people. To go through any formation program successfully, we had to become foreigners to our own people, we had to abandon the very sources of our faith and the deepest bonding of *nuestro pueblo*. No wonder that over half of the ordained Mexican American priests at that time did not want to work with Mexican American people. This couple's simple word from the heart immediately revealed to me why I had felt a certain anger and disgust within me at the theological formation that had turned me against my people and especially against the very expressions of the faith through which I had come to know and love God, Jesus, Mary, and the saints in a very personal way. I had never verbalized this, even to myself. But this was the naked truth: theology had caused me to abandon rather than understand the living faith tradition of my people. This was a betrayal both of theology itself and of my people's faith. Paradoxical as it sounds, theological formation had made me and others like me dishonor our parents and ancestors; it had made us break the fourth commandment. Our theological formation was preparing us to destroy the faith basis of our Mexican American existence.

It was at this moment that I, as a diocesan priest who had never been too interested in academic or university theology, decided that either we ourselves must begin to theologize seriously out of the living faith experience of our people, or theology would continue to alienate Mexican American priests and religious from our own people and thus damage our people's faith.

— "Hispanic Theology and Popular Piety," 2–3

SURVIVING INJUSTICE

Virgilio was ordained a priest for the San Antonio archdiocese on May 25, 1963. His early pastoral assignments within the San Antonio archdiocese included Our Lady of Sorrows parish in San Antonio, St. Mary's in Stockdale, and Sacred Heart in Floresville, where the following incident occurred.

I can well remember one of my early assignments as a priest while Lyndon B. Johnson was president. The whole country was excited about initiating programs that eliminate poverty. It was a fantastic dream. I was stationed in a small country parish and tried to establish a youth program that would pay minimum wages while the youth were in training for future jobs. When the program was about to start, some of the Mexican American leadership of the town came to speak with me. To my great amazement, they asked me to drop the program.

I could not believe what I was hearing. Crazy thoughts went quickly through my mind: Were they jealous that their children were going to get a good wage? Didn't they trust me? Didn't they want their children to get ahead? Maybe they just liked being poor and didn't want to change!

Then they started to explain. The Mexican Americans in that area worked for about one-third the minimum wage. Yet the whole area was controlled by the large landowners. As long as the people did not make trouble, they were safe to enjoy their simple life. But if they started to work for any change in the status quo, one or two members of the Mexican American community would simply disappear. They loved the program I wanted to bring into the area, but they did not want to disturb the status quo at the cost of their children's disappearance. So for the time being we dropped the program. There are many ways of keeping a people down and the fear of losing a loved one is one of the most effective.

It is true that sometimes people accept situations because they are afraid of risks or too lazy to take the initiative. Yet it is equally true that in certain circumstances the wise and prudent natural leaders of the people know from experience that the only option open for them to survive and to prepare for the ultimate liberation of the people is to accept the situation as it is and make the best of it. To accept it does not mean we like it or enjoy it; it is simply a way of coping with it in order to survive.

— *The Future Is Mestizo*, 30–31

GOD AMONG THE FARM WORKERS

Virgilio's friendship with César Chávez and involvement with the farm worker struggle profoundly shaped his ministry and spirituality. A widely admired labor organizer and leader whose faith animated his activism, César Estrada Chávez (1927–1993) was born near Yuma, Arizona, and moved with his family to California in 1939. There he followed in his parents' footsteps, laboring as a farm worker in the San Joaquin Valley. During the 1960s, he collaborated with Dolores Huerta to establish the National Farm Workers Association (later known as the United

Farm Workers), the first union to secure contracts and official recognition from California growers. Despite initial reluctance from Catholic bishops and priests, the union leaders also garnered support from church and civic leaders. The following excerpt presents involvement with the farm workers as an experience of God and their struggle as a divine call for conversion and action. It shows that one privileged means we encounter God is in the cries of victims and their fight for justice.

Another great experience of God came through the farm worker movement led by César Chávez, especially in California and Texas. The poor Mexicans in the United States had never been allowed the protection of labor laws. In effect, unions and labor legislation kept saying: Mexican (and other) farm workers do not count in the United States. Migrant workers were constantly brought in from Mexico as needed and then sent back to keep the local farm workers from unionizing.

These *campesinos* were forced to work under the most brutal and dehumanizing circumstances — under the scorching sun, constantly stooped down to pick the crops, without toilets or water. Even worse, often the crops were fumigated with dangerous chemicals while the workers and their babies were in the fields. They were paid less than the minimum wage for seasonal work and received no workers' benefits whatsoever. I am sure that the slaves in Egypt did not have it any worse than our poor farm workers.

César Chávez, a poor farm worker himself, called for nonviolent crusades. The Mexican victims took the lead. People throughout the country were asked to boycott the buying of grapes and lettuce. All the big landowners and labor unions were against them. Many tried to discredit them and even threatened them in many ways. It is said that when the grape boycott was really beginning to take effect across the country, the dietitians at the Pentagon decided that grapes were very good for the soldiers in Asia so eight pounds of grapes per soldier per day were sent to Asia! It was like David against Goliath.

César Chávez dared to reveal the hideous and unjust structures which were kept in place to assure the success of a few at the cost of sacrificing the many on the altars of the crop picking fields. The human sacrifices continued, but they had been nicely and politely camouflaged and hidden. America could enjoy its good fruits and vegetables without having to think about the body and blood sacrifices that were required to get the food onto the tables. Yet the campaign continued and brought some moderate changes. It still continues while the opposition grows more grotesque each day.

All the powers conspired to destroy the defenseless movement of the victimized farm workers. On the other hand, the more the resistance grew, the more men and women of all backgrounds and religious persuasions started to join the crusade. As in the civil rights movement, there were Jews, Christians, and others; Protestants and Catholics; religious and laity; whites, blacks, and browns. No one had any problem marching behind the banner of Our Lady of Guadalupe for she was the traditional protectress of the Mexican poor and their banner in their struggles for justice. We sang religious songs and prayed the rosary. We were together and united, and the more we were threatened, the more we knew God was with us. Marching with the farm workers was a rewalking of the way of the cross. Those who took part, regardless of their religious persuasion, knew they had truly experienced God present among us.

The civil rights movements and the farm worker movement have brought us into solidarity with the other suffering victims of the Americas in their struggles for new life. They are beginning to see themselves as the suffering servant. It is not God's will to bruise them. As in the Exodus, God is present in the struggles of the oppressed "nobodies" against the unjust oppression of Pharaoh, and the gods of the empire are powerless against the God who hears the cries of the poor. As in the crucifixion, God speaks absolute truth from the position and through the lips of the crucified ones whom God will resurrect. The resurrected peoples of the Americas are the ones who will usher in the truly new humanity of the Americas. They are the people of hope.

These movements are not asking for revolutions, but for the conversion of all: of the poor from their passive and silent suffering, of the dominant from their arrogance and blindness. The call of our society's victims is like the call of Jesus to the rich young man. God is speaking to all of us through the cries of today's suffering servants. Will we listen?

— "Evil and the Experience of God," 40–42

MESTIZO SOUL

The following incident, which Virgilio frequently recounts as a core moment in his life and the development of his thought, launched his spiritual explorations of mestizaje *and its significance in his life and that of his fellow Mexican Americans.*

In 1967, Father Francisco Aguilera, a Mexican *mestizo* who was comfortable and proud of both his Spanish and Amerindian ancestry, took me to visit the Plaza de las Tres Culturas in Mexico City where the final battles between the Aztecs and the Spaniards took place. On this sacred ground where a colonial church sits upon the ruins of the old pyramid-Temples and is surrounded by modern-day apartment houses, there is an inscription that reads:

> *On this site*
> *on the sad night of August 13, 1521*
> *heroically taken by Cortés*
> *valiantly defended by Cuauhtemoc*
> *it was neither a defeat nor a victory*
> *but the painful birth of the* mestizo *people*
> *which is México today.*

We then went to visit Our Lady of Guadalupe. I had been there before, but this was a totally new experience as Father

Aguilera explained to me how in and through her, the Iberian soul had united with the ancient Mexican soul to give rise to the *mestizo* soul of Mexico. This was the ongoing miracle of Guadalupe, this is what truly made her the Mother of the Americas, because she had given birth and continues to give birth to the new people of the Americas.

This was the beginning of a real rebirth for me, a coming to grips with the innermost reality of my being and that of my people. I immediately realized that what had appeared as "nonbeing" was in reality the beginning of new being. The carnal and spiritual borders of identity and belonging had been pierced, the geographical/historical being of "the other" had been penetrated, and a new being had been conceived and born who would be fully both and something new. I quickly reread the Alamo story* through the same categories — not of defeat or victory, but of birth — the birth of a people, the birth of a soul, the birth of a spirituality, the birth of a church, and the birth of a religion. I could be proud of my collective grandparents: Iberia and pre-Columbian Mexico, and I could equally be proud of my parent cultures: WASPish United States and *mestizo* Catholic Mexico.

— "Transformation of Borders," 26–27

ESTABLISHING A PASTORAL CENTER

Shortly after his ordination, Virgilio served as director of religious education for the San Antonio archdiocese and as the academic dean of the archdiocese's Assumption Seminary. Fascinated with the recent Second Vatican Council, especially its

---

*The 1836 Alamo battle occurred in Virgilio's hometown of San Antonio. The site remains a popular tourist attraction hailed as "the shrine of Texas liberty." Most visitors perceive the Alamo as a memorial to the valor of Anglo-American defenders against their Mexican attackers, though at least nine Alamo defenders were Mexicans born in Texas, or Tejanos. Virgilio sees the Alamo as a symbolic reference point for the painful encounter of the peoples of Mexico and the United States that formed his Mexican American people.

pastoral vision and call to a return to the sources of faith, he also established the Pastoral Institute at San Antonio's Incarnate Word College (now the University of the Incarnate Word) to form pastoral and catechetical leaders. In 1969, he completed a master's degree in pastoral studies from the Ateneo University and a diploma in pastoral catechetics from the East Asian Pastoral Institute, both in Manila. His experiences in pastoral leadership formation and his desire to serve his own struggling people enabled one of his most renowned initiatives: the 1972 founding of the Mexican American Cultural Center (MACC, now the Mexican American Catholic College), which he subsequently served as its first president until 1987. The following selection is from an essay Virgilio wrote for a journal issue commemorating the twenty-fifth anniversary of MACC.

The "why" of the Mexican American Cultural Center is quite simple: many of us native-born, Spanish-speaking Catholics were frustrated and even angered at the very church we loved and had committed our lives to because it was not ministering to our people. Although over 25 percent of Catholics in the United States were Spanish-speaking, there was no real recognition of, respect for, or ministry to the Latino Catholic of the United States. Yet we did not just want to complain. We wanted to do something ourselves. What emerged is today the Mexican American Cultural Center.

How did the Mexican American Cultural Center come about? How did it succeed so instantaneously? How did it gain such grassroots and worldwide credibility so fast? It wasn't a university, yet it posed profound academic questions. It wasn't simply a pastoral center, yet it addressed the most immediate and deepest questions of pastoral activity. It wasn't an ordinary institution of the church, yet it was involved in the most pertinent questions and struggles of Vatican II. How did all this come about?

There were three defining moments which gave birth to the Mexican American Cultural Center. The first and most dramatic was the first National Retreat of PADRES (Priests Associated for

Religious, Educational, and Social Rights) conducted by Scripture professor John Linskens, C.I.C.M., of the East Asian Pastoral Institute in the Philippines, which was held at the seminary in Santa Fe, New Mexico, in February 1972. In the midst of this challenge to strive to produce our own cultural-linguistic interpretation of the Scriptures, and a need to prepare our own people to do this, the idea erupted almost spontaneously, almost as a divine mandate: since there were so few of us (native-born priests, religious, and lay leaders) we needed to concentrate our efforts on bringing our experts together in one place. Hence, we needed to create that place, a pastoral center. Here we could come together to research who we *frontera* (frontier) people were from within our own geographic historic reality: to study the Scriptures, worship, and church life; to form our own leaders and others who wanted to work with our people; to teach others about our language and culture; to publish materials to support our work. It was a great idea. How to get this going was now the challenge! Las Hermanas, under the dynamic leadership of Sisters María de Jesús Ybarra and Camelita Espinosa, immediately helped to get the enterprise started.

The second defining moment came during the general annual assembly of the Texas Catholic Conference in Austin in September of 1972. Two vocation directors, Tom Syte of San Angelo and Ron Anderson of Brownsville, had become fascinated with the idea of the founding of such a pastoral center. They wanted to help us turn it into a reality. Syte and Anderson took the PADRES proposal and presented it to the assembly.

It took no convincing. The assembly was aware of the needs and liked the comprehensiveness of the proposal. There was great enthusiasm: no one wanted to wait, and it became the main item on the agenda. Archbishop Furey [of San Antonio] appointed a steering committee to convert the proposal into a reality. Everyone agreed that there was no time to waste.

The third defining moment came when, meeting in the library of Assumption Seminary, the steering committee decided effectively to create what would become known as the Mexican

American Cultural Center, popularly called MACC. The committee prepared the constitution and bylaws, appointed a board
(with Bishop Patrick Flores as its chairperson), applied for a
state charter, and named myself as the first director. Where
would the center be located? Archbishop Furey offered the
unused section of Assumption Seminary. The board accepted
his offer to rent it for $1.00 per year. Thus MACC was born.
It was conceived in New Mexico, implanted in the womb of
Austin, Texas, and delivered in the library of Assumption Seminary in San Antonio. The baby was born and launched on a life
of its own.

— "The Mexican American Cultural Center Story," 152–54

ANCESTRAL ROOTS

*Under Virgilio's leadership, MACC quickly took on a cru-
cial national role in forming pastoral leaders, advocating for
Hispanic ministry and rights, and publishing groundbreaking
research about Hispanic liturgy, faith expressions, history, and
theology. For the first time, Mexican American priests, sisters, and lay leaders, along with some other collaborators,
had an institution of their own to explore their heritage and
develop insights such as the theological and pastoral implications of their experience as* mestizos *living between two
cultures. The following excerpt highlights the exhilarating sense
of self-discovery and the urgency to learn more and bring good
news to their people that many have taken away from their
experiences at MACC.*

As we started to struggle for freedom and equality within society, we also started to ask deeper questions about ourselves,
about our families, about our heritage, about our past. It was
not sufficient to become a professional or to get rich. We needed
much more. We had been marginalized not just because we

were poor but because we were Mexican. But we were not Mexican citizens. We were fully U.S.-Americans, just as much as anyone else. Yet there was something definitely distinct about us. Just who were we? Where did we come from? Why were we the way we were?

We needed answers, not to apologize to anyone for who we were, but to know ourselves. Our schools had never taught us about ourselves: our literature, our history, our customs, our traditions, our food. We had studied about everyone else but never about ourselves. Our story had been either totally absent or completely misrepresented by the history books of the schools, universities, and seminaries. Latin American church history was totally missing from the learned tomes of church history, as if it didn't even exist, even though 50 percent of the entire Catholic Church is in Latin America.

All of a sudden we had discovered a fascinating new entity — ourselves. Before, we had lived our identity in silence and solitude, almost as if we were not supposed to be. We had sheepishly apologized, joked, ignored. But now we could be. We could study ourselves and our origins. We could openly celebrate our traditions and speak about ourselves from within our own experience. We had discovered that in order to truly affirm ourselves, we had to be able to retell our story — the story of the great pilgrimage of our ancestors that had led us to be who we are today. So we started to go seriously into our past, and what a fascinating and liberating revelation it would prove to be. History is not merely the record of the past but the life-source of the present and the hidden energy for the new future.

As a people, we had been born as a result of the U.S. invasion and subsequent conquest of the great northern regions of Mexico from California to Texas. And before that our Mexican ancestors had been born out of the invasion and conquest of pre-Columbian Mexico. As the Spanish conquest of Mexico had tried to suppress everything native, so the Anglo conquest of northern Mexico had tried to suppress and destroy everything Mexican. We could say that in recent historical times, we

had been twice conquered, twice victimized, and twice mesti-
cized. Through each conquest, the native soil with its culture
and inhabitants had been deeply penetrated but not destroyed.
The conquerors had tried to destroy the natives, but in time
they would be absorbed and conquered by the product of their
own unsuspected creation. Like the womb of a woman receiv-
ing the seed of a man to produce new life, so in Mexico and
subsequently in the Southwest of today's United States, a new
child had been conceived and born.

We needed to know our parents in order to know who we
were. We knew the U.S.-American side. In the classrooms and
in the movies, we had learned well about the great experiment
in democracy, about the Boston Tea Party and the rebellion
against taxation without representation, about the American
war of independence in 1776, about the constitutional conven-
tion, and about the birth of the great republic of the United
States of America. Its historical development had been as fascinating as it had been ambiguous. We had learned about the
greatness of the American experience and we held it in great
reverence. What we had not studied were the cruel injustices
involved in the process of nation building: the massacres of the
natives, the slave trade, the systematic impoverishment of the
Mexican inhabitants of the Southwest.

So now we started to discover the treasures of ancient Mexico. Our school books had always spoken about the Indians as
backward savages. What an illuminating discovery to find that
our ancient Mexican ancestors from New Mexico to the valley of Anahuac were highly sophisticated and civilized peoples
whose scientific achievements were in many ways far ahead
of European civilization: medicine, art, philosophy, architec-
ture, commerce, education, astronomy, agriculture. Many of
our common foods today are of native origins: chocolate, toma-
toes, potatoes, chile beans, corn, turkeys. The ways of life were
humanizing: proper upbringing of the young people, respect for
the elders and their ways, respect for the dignity of the other.

— *The Future Is Mestizo*, 38–41

RENEWING THE SOUL OF THE CITY

Virgilio served as rector of San Antonio's renowned San Fernando Cathedral from 1983 to 1995, concurrently continuing his work as president of MACC for the first four years of his pastorship. During his tenure at San Fernando he led the predominately Mexican American congregation in a revival of their faith traditions. One of the most prominent celebrations was the vigil for the December 12 feast of Our Lady of Guadalupe, for which Virgilio initiated a serenata celebration of songs to Guadalupe transmitted throughout the Americas via television. He rejuvenated the congregation's practice of a public proclamation of Jesus' passion and death on Good Friday, drawing tens of thousands for the annual commemoration beginning in the public market, winding through the city's downtown streets, and ending with the crucifixion on the steps of the cathedral. Virgilio also established the internationally televised Misa de las Americas, *which the San Fernando congregation celebrated weekly with millions participating via television. The following excerpt reflects Virgilio's vision of the public role of a cathedral that guided his initiatives and leadership at San Fernando.*

In 1983, the archbishop of San Antonio [Patricio Flores] offered me a totally unsuspected opportunity, a position as rector of the cathedral. Immediately, my heart started to spin with memories, ideas, possibilities, and dreams. The archbishop had been working with me at the Mexican American Cultural Center (MACC) in San Antonio, where our team of scholars and pastoral ministers explored our Mexican American reality and how to formulate creative pastoral responses to the growing needs of our people. He prefaced his invitation with the statement, "Now is the chance to prove that what you have been saying needs to be done. Let's show what our people have to offer."

I listened, consulted, and prayed, yet in the back of my mind and heart, I had accepted the archbishop's invitation the moment he mentioned it. This appointment as rector was an opportunity to dream, to motivate, and to create. Some of my close friends and colleagues had encouraged me to continue my research and writing at MACC, where I had been for the last fifteen years. They had also noted that "anyone" could serve as rector at the cathedral, which appeared to be a dying parish of elderly people.

But I saw unlimited possibilities and accepted. When I began to meet the people, I immediately fell in love with each of them. It was like coming home to a long-lost family that welcomed me with open arms. It seemed like I had known them all my life and, indeed, many of them had even carried me in their arms as a baby or scolded me when I was a young boy running around the cathedral.

Besides a homecoming, my arrival in 1983 as rector was also a rebirth. I was the first native-born San Antonian to be named rector of the cathedral. The parish was my intimate family, yet I had a new and deeper perception and appreciation of San Fernando, San Antonio, its geographical location, its history, its people, and its fascinating potential. I made a conscious decision to reclaim and re-create the religious traditions of my childhood and of my barrio as the basis for the pastoral life of the cathedral. This was not because of nostalgia but out of a conviction that these sacred traditions were not only the basis of our faith experience as Latinos and our innermost identity as a people, but that they were desperately needed for the spiritual health and salvation of the United States.

Daily for the next twelve years San Fernando was where I worked and struggled. Each day I discovered more about the incredible architectural, historical, and living treasures within its walls and surroundings. The people who come to San Fernando became my closest friends and greatest teachers. Their infused sense of reverence, ritual, and devotion is both fascinating and captivating. Today, the spiritual energy of this living mystery goes far beyond the walls of the cathedral. Through our weekly televised Mass, millions from all backgrounds and denominations throughout the Americas join together in experiencing the presence of God through our rituals and fellowship. Where does this spiritual energy come from?

As I celebrated the early predawn daily Mass during any given day of the week, I felt always that we were energizing the entire city of San Antonio for one more day. As I offered the Holy Sacrifice, I felt that I was in continuity with Jesus, who sacrificed himself to give us life, and with our Aztec ancestors, who offered predawn sacrifices to ensure that the sun would rise another day. I was in continuity with the generations from time immemorial who struggled and sacrificed to make this space of earth a more hospitable home for anyone who comes here. It was like "fueling up" the spiritual engines that give life to our city.

In the tranquility of the daily liturgies, I felt in contact with my most ancient and even primal roots, with everyone in my city and the world, and with the generations to come until the end of time. San Fernando gave me the strength of experiencing the continuum of life. It was a mystical experience of continuity and transformation, of tradition and renewal, of death and resurrection. Never before had the words "Christ has died, Christ has risen, Christ will come again" taken on such real meaning as they did during these early predawn celebrations of the Holy Sacrifice.

Whether in the quiet of the early morning Mass or in the packed-like-sardines crowds of the noon Mass on Sundays or the massive faith demonstrations of Holy Week, anyone who comes to San Fernando experiences God in a very special way. As so many have told us, here God is alive and present.

As cathedrals were the unifying center of old European cities, so did San Fernando Cathedral become the unifying center, the soul, of San Antonio. My hope was that it would be a *mestizo* cathedral that would extend far beyond our own Mexican American *mestizaje*. My goal was to unite, synthesize, and enrich various religious traditions into one coherent whole. San Fernando would become the *cathedra,* the teaching chair, from which we would learn about ourselves as the image and likeness of God and joyfully celebrate our new awareness of ourselves.

European cathedrals quickly became the centers of joyful celebrations of a redeemed humanity. This had to be a key element at San Fernando. People and clergy had to celebrate together. In the fiesta city of San Antonio, our cathedral had to be festive. We involved artists, musicians, dancers, poets, actors, vendors, festival organizers, decorators, radio, television, and the press to open up the Word of God to the masses. They all became pastoral agents of San Fernando as the cathedral strived to become a twenty-four-hour liturgical celebration of humanity.

Given the rise of secular society with its massive skyscrapers that dwarf even the greatest of cathedrals, I wondered if cathedrals could ever again play a privileged role in city and society. And my questioning went even deeper. Can the city of God exist in the very center of the cities of men and women today? Can there be a sacred space that is made sacred precisely because it violates all human barriers of division, because it dares to bring together all peoples so that they may see each other, care for one another, and work together? This must happen if we are to transform our cities from the present-day battlefields into human spaces where people can live, walk, work, and have fun in peace and harmony. We *can* learn from the past to reclaim this beautiful tradition of God as the light and center of all human activity.   — *San Fernando Cathedral,* 9–13

HOMECOMING

While his ministry, teaching, and scholarship have taken him to places all around the world, Virgilio has lived in his hometown and neighborhood almost all his life. Reflecting his own life journey of itinerancy and homecoming, the following selection presents Virgilio's thoughts on our human longing for home, for our roots, and ultimately for God.

My mother immigrated to the United States from Mexico at a very young age. She and her mother came from Mexico City by train. She learned to love the United States and never talked about returning to Mexico. During the rest of her life, she had very little contact with Mexico, except for visits from relatives who occasionally visited my hometown of San Antonio. Yet during her final days on earth she became nostalgic about returning to Mexico City by train. Sometimes I would come home in the evening and she would be anxious about going to take the train to Mexico. The only way I could calm her down was to tell her today's train had already left, but we could go the next day. In her dying days she was anxious to return to the place of her origins.

It is beautiful to see how during major holidays or personal events such as weddings, baptisms, and funerals people are eager to return home to be reunited not only with family and friends but also with the landscape and familiar surroundings of the homestead. Immigrants who come to the United States from Mexico, the Philippines, Vietnam, and other countries often make great sacrifices to return home for special events and even just vacations. Often immigrants like to place a bit of the old sod in their new country by building churches like they had in the old country, opening restaurants that serve their traditional food, and organizing celebrations like they had back home. Ethnic food sections have become very popular in the grocery stores of our multiethnic America. Sometimes immigrants want their bodies returned home for burial after they die. Even if they had left because of misery and horrible conditions, they still often speak sentimentally of the home country as a lost paradise. People whose ancestors immigrated to new lands generations ago are often nostalgic about making a visit to the "home country."

I remember a good friend of mine who is a university professor making a trip to the small town in northern Italy from which his grandparents had emigrated. He was totally "Americanized," yet he felt an inner calling to visit the land of his origins. He didn't know any Italian, and it probably would not have helped him if he did because in that small town people spoke a dialect quite unique to the mountain area between Italy and Austria. Yet when he arrived, he managed to communicate and actually find elderly people who remembered his family and were able to take him to the home where his father had been born. They even went to the local parish and found his baptismal record. I remember visiting with him upon his return, and the excitement that he exhibited was beyond the words he could find to explain it, even though he was a very popular conference presenter who was never at a loss for words. He said he really could not explain the deep feeling of being connected with what seemed like ultimate reality, like being connected to the very roots of his existence.

Even though I very much know San Antonio as my hometown, I remember very well the first time we visited the small hamlet where my father had been born and raised in northern Mexico and then when we visited my mother's birthplace in the great and ancient metropolitan capital that is Mexico City. The contrast between the small hamlet and the glowing capital was striking, yet the deep feeling of returning to the place of my origins was equally profound, nostalgic, and even sacred in both places. I knew instinctively without anyone having to explain it to me that I was in contact with the earthly origins of my existence. Was this an expression of a desire for something much greater and primordial?

It is no wonder that "homecoming" celebrations are major attractions that bring people from distant places, while restaurants like to promote the fact that they serve home-cooked meals. As we grow up, especially in today's world of easy and quick mobility, we go in many directions, finding new friends and forming new networks of relationships. Yet there is something deep within us that secretly longs to be united with our origins, with our roots, with the ground of our existence. Even if we had difficult experiences growing up, there is still a spark buried deep within our psyche that pulls us toward the place of our origins.

It seems that it is within our very makeup that we have the need to be connected to that from which we have come, to be in touch with our earthly roots. Could this quest for origins be indicative of something much greater than we dare imagine? Could it be the whisper of our desire to be in contact with the ultimate root of our existence and eventually be reunited with our origins? I remember both my father and mother in their final moments calling out to their mothers, to the womb that had given them life, and their dying desire to be reunited with this place of origin.

We come from God who is love, the source of goodness and beauty, and our final destiny is to be reunited with God in love.

— *Charity*, 103–5

2

Gospel Dynamics

Galilee must have been of special salvific signification to the first Christians, since it plays an important role in the post-Easter memory of the followers of Jesus and becomes part of the earliest kerygma (Acts 10:37–41).... Why is Jesus' ethnic identity as a Jewish Galilean from Nazareth an important dimension of the incarnation, and what does it disclose about the beauty and originality of Jesus' liberating life and message?
— "Jesus the Galilean Jew in Mestizo Theology," 270

Mexican Americans' devotion to Christ complements their well-known veneration of Our Lady of Guadalupe. The U.S. Catholic bishops stated in their 1983 pastoral, The Hispanic Presence: Challenge and Commitment: *"Hispanic spirituality places strong emphasis on the humanity of Jesus, especially when he appears weak and suffering, as in the crib and in his passion and death" (no. 12). During the nine days before Christmas,* posadas *(literally "dwellings") reenact Mary and Joseph's pilgrimage to Bethlehem. The* acostada *and* levantada del niño *celebration — literally "laying down" and "taking up the child" — entails a solemn enthronement and later removal of the child Jesus from the nativity scene. On Good Friday, rituals include a public reenactment of Jesus' trial, way of the cross, and crucifixion, or an outdoor way of the cross procession. Evening services can include traditions such as the* servicio del santo entierro, *or entombment of Jesus taken down from the cross, and the* pésame, *a wake service for Jesus with condolences offered to La Dolorosa, his sorrowful mother.*

Virgilio's writings accentuate these core moments in Jesus' life and in Hispanic spirituality. He underscores the scandal of the incarnation, how unexpectedly human God became in Jesus of Galilee. Yet he insists that the human and vulnerable Jesus seen as a child and in agony dying on the cross and the resurrected Christ who shatters the reign of evil are one and the same person. Our search for understanding must examine the entirety of the Christ event and the mystery of Christ.

Virgilio's longstanding attraction to the Gospel narratives, the struggles for dignity of his own Mexican American people, and the call of the Second Vatican Council to return to the foundational sources of the faith were the seeds of his quest to explore the Gospel dynamics and their implications for discipleship today. Jesus' birth as a Galilean discloses from the outset that God's solidarity with the lowly is revealed in him. From the angel Gabriel's announcement of his conception in Mary's womb to the sending of the Holy Spirit at Pentecost, Jesus bursts into the lives of those the world rejects and proclaims that God rejects no one. He confronts the powers of exclusion and rejection at their source. He endures the cross rather than give in to the vengeful human tendency of responding in kind to rejection and violence. In his resurrection and Pentecost dawn the hope that God's love triumphs over the sin of the world. Collectively the selections in this chapter address not a generic but a particular examination of Jesus: How would we understand and live the Gospels if we took seriously the biblical witness to Jesus' Galilean origins?

THE GALILEAN INSIGHT

On his return from attending the meeting of Latin American bishops at Medellín in 1968, Virgilio had a chance meeting on the airplane with another Medellín attendee, Fr. Jacques Audinet, professor of practical theology at the Institut Catholique de Paris. That conversation began a lifelong friendship, including Audinet's encouragement that Virgilio pursue doctoral studies at the Institut Catholique, which he subsequently did, completing his thesis entitled "Métissage, violence culturelle, annonce de l'Evangile" *under Audinet's direction in 1978. In Paris Virgilio developed the central question of his meditations on Jesus of Nazareth: Why Galilee? If God's Son could have been born in any time and place, what is the significance of his taking flesh as a Galilean Jew? What light does Jesus' Galilean identity shed on our understanding of his public ministry, table fellowship, and eventual passion, death, and resurrection?*

Later, because of my work at MACC [the Mexican American Cultural Center], I was invited to do doctoral studies at the Institut Catholique de Paris, where I had the good fortune to study historical theology with Marie Dominique Chenu, O.P., ecclesiology with Yves Congar, O.P., sociology and theology with Jacques Audinet, *nouvelle théologie* with Claude Gefre, O.P., and René Marlé, S.J., and patristic theology and methods for actualizing the word of God with Charles Kannengiesser, S.J. In Paris I learned that all theological reflection, consciously or not, is socially and culturally situated. Our social situation gives us a unique perspective, and when we come together in communion and dialogue, the perspectives of each enriches the entire church. It is not a question of placing one theology against another, but of bringing them together as various beautiful pieces of one mosaic.

Against this background, I formulated my theological frame of reference: (1) study and present the historical, social, and religious situation of the people as the arena for the work of both sin and grace; (2) read the Gospel matrix from our socio-cultural situation; and (3) read the culture in light of the Gospel in order to discern the meaning of the word of God today. This approach would bring out aspects of the Gospel we had not anticipated and uncover aspects of the historical-cultural situation we ourselves had missed. The idea was to "submit to a new scrutiny the deeds and words which God has revealed" [*Ad Gentes,* no. 22] so that the faith of the people might develop a more complete self-understanding.

In writing my doctoral thesis in Paris (1976–78), it was not difficult to put together the historical, cultural, and religious sections. I had been gathering material and developing the key concepts with our interdisciplinary and interethnic team at the Mexican American Cultural Center for several years. The historical context would be the twofold conquest and colonization: first Spain's conquest of today's Latin America, and then the U.S. conquest of the northern region of Mexico. This historical process had produced our *mestizaje* with deep contemporary problems of identity and belonging rooted in marginalization — and sometimes total exclusion — from both parent groups. It was from within this perspective that I began to search the Gospels for the Christian meaning of our quest.

The great theologies I studied and loved were fascinating but still distant, and they offered no theological understanding of the *mestizo* reality of our living faith. What did the Gospel have to offer our people? Could the Gospel help us understand the deeper meaning of our historical process and culture? In what ways did the Gospel bring healing and empowerment to Mexican American people in the context of an Anglo-American culture that marginalized and excluded us? Some scriptural concepts started to emerge as programmatic: the rejected "suffering servant" and the "new heaven and new earth" of Isaiah's universalism; Philippians' total self-emptying of the Son; the kingdom of God wherein all are welcomed; the positive dealings

of Jesus with the "impure" and "excluded"; and the decla-
ration that "the stone rejected by the builders has become
the cornerstone" (Matt. 21:42, Mark 12:10, Luke 20:17, Acts
4:11, 1 Pet. 2:7). Since the New Testament asserts that Jesus
brings about a new creation, I wondered if the "stone rejected"
becoming the cornerstone of the new creation might not be a
critical allusion to the builders of unjust and arrogant societies
harkening back to the Tower of Babel (Gen. 11) — the very
ones rejected by them would become the foundation stones of
the new!

In praying over Scripture and reading through various theological and biblical journals in light of the fascination of our
people with the earthly (carnal) *Jesús Nazareno,* a question
emerged, a curiosity at first, as to why the constant mention of
Galilee in the Gospel narratives was not, as far as I could see,
a contemporary theological point of reference? More than sixty
times the Gospels mention "Galilee," "Galileans," and places
in Galilee. Luke places the Annunciation (1:26–38) and the
beginning of the public ministry of Jesus in Galilee (4:14–21).
Mark places "the beginning of the good news of Jesus Christ"
there (1:1, 9), along with the majority of his ministry. In three
Gospels the risen Lord sends the disciples to Galilee, where they
will see him (Matt. 28:7; Mark 16:7; John 21:1); Luke does
not send them back to Galilee, but at Pentecost the speakers are
identified as Galileans (Acts 2:7).

In Galilee Peter is commissioned to be the leader of the new
flock (John 21:15–17), and from Galilee the disciples are sent to
all nations and to the ends of the earth (Matt. 28:16–20). Given
the importance of Jerusalem to Jewish restoration thinking at
the time, I wondered why Galilee had become such an important point of reference in the Gospels. Galilee seemed of little
or no importance in the Hebrew Bible and had apparently negative connotations for some of the people at the time of Jesus
(Matt. 21:10–11; John 1:46, 49; 7:52). It seemed to me that
Galilee must have been of special salvific signification to the first
Christians, since it plays an important role in the post-Easter

memory of the followers of Jesus and becomes part of the earliest kerygma (Acts 10:37–41). The question pressed itself: Why is Jesus' ethnic identity as a Jewish Galilean from Nazareth an important dimension of the incarnation, and what does it disclose about the beauty and originality of Jesus' liberating life and message?

In one of the few references found in the Hebrew Bible, the prophet Isaiah (8:23) refers to "Galilee of the Gentiles." Isaiah also speaks of universal salvation for all the nations, of a new era of peace and harmony, and even of a new heaven and a new earth. The influence of Isaiah's perspective in the New Testament seemed to suggest a unique and unsuspected role for Galilee in God's salvific plan for the restoration of unity among the human family, a unity and harmony that had been destroyed by sin since the very beginning of creation (Gen. 3–11). The relative unimportance of Galilee seemed to fit with the idea that the Gospel is absurd to many, that the ways of God appear as foolishness to the wise of this world, and that the redemptive grace of God is an unexpected gift.

— "Jesus the Galilean Jew in Mestizo Theology," 268–71

THE SISTERHOOD
OF THE VISITATION

Virgilio's focus is not primarily on interpreting the meaning of the Gospels as ancient texts, but on engaging the Gospels through the experience of Mexican Americans and simultaneously interpreting their experience in light of the imagery and narratives of the Gospels. The following excerpt comes from his most extensive publication of Gospel meditations, his 2003 book A God of Incredible Surprises: Jesus of Galilee. *It underscores that God's revelation in the Christ event begins with the faith and courage of the peasant woman Mary of Nazareth, who bore Jesus in her womb. The eyes of faith enable*

Elizabeth to recognize the blessedness of God in her hum-
ble kinswoman from Galilee. This selection shows that being
deeply attentive to others, particularly the poor and those who
are suffering, illuminates God's Word through the prism of their
experience.

Mary goes to visit her cousin Elizabeth. When her cousin recognizes that the one Mary carries within her womb is of God,
immediately Mary rejoices and proclaims one of the most beautiful and powerful hymns found in the New Testament: "My
soul proclaims the greatness of the Lord" (Luke 1:46). What
others might look upon as a disgrace and a scandal, a baby out
of wedlock, Elizabeth recognizes what every new life truly is:
a gift of God! I have known of similar cases in which a violated woman was insulted in the most horrible terms by her
own family as she was being driven from the family home,
only to be taken in by a loving grandmother, aunt, or home
for unwed mothers who rebuilt the dignity of the woman by
welcoming her with kindness, treating her with dignity, praying
with her, and assuring her that regardless of the circumstances
of the beginning, rape or a mistake on her part, life is from
God and that her child could be, as Jesus was, destined to be
the savior of many people. I know one very good and effective priest today who came exactly out of these circumstances.
His mother's family wanted her to have an abortion because she
had conceived out of wedlock. At the last moment, she backed
away and gave birth to a healthy child. The child became her
life. He had difficulty being welcomed into a seminary because
of his illegitimate status. Finally, he found a religious order that
would accept him. He has accomplished wonders in his work
as a priest.

No one fully understands the mysteries of God's ways, even
in the conception of life. There is the normal way of conception, which is beautiful and holy, but even when conception has
taken place in a different way, the child is still of God and a
blessing for humanity. And the woman who conceived, even if

she had been the most sinful of all, is still not rejected by God, for God rejects the sin but not the sinner. The sinner is not condemned but rather invited to experience the boundless mercy of a loving, understanding, and forgiving God.

In this sense, Elizabeth is the first one to proclaim the good news. Men (like Joseph) are scandalized, but women (like Elizabeth) understood and praised God. What had appeared to be a human story of pain and scandal, even to good Joseph, is now recognized and proclaimed for the great blessing that it truly is: "Most blessed are you among women and blessed is the fruit of your womb" (Luke 1:42). Thus it is not only the women who first proclaim the resurrection, but it is a woman who first recognizes the presence of God in the child in the womb of an unwed mother. It is the holiness of this woman that allows her to see reality for what it truly is: not a scandal but a great blessing. And the woman who others might be scandalized by is proclaimed for what every mother truly is: "Blessed." Every woman who is a carrier of new life is blessed, for during her pregnancy she is cooperating with God in a very special way in the creation of new life. It is the sinful eyes that cannot recognize life as a blessing and would not hesitate to get rid of the mother and the child. Yet the one who in her time was a scandal according to the sinful categories of judgment would be called blessed by all generations to come who in the new creation began to see not as sinful humanity sees, but as God sees.

— *A God of Incredible Surprises*, 29–31

SALVATION OF THE SHEPHERDS

Many of Virgilio's most creative spiritual insights are not published on the printed page. His homilies and numerous public presentations and workshops provide potent memories for numerous listeners who have experienced him at his best: when he is interacting with people and building on the spirit of the *group. The following selection from a Christmas homily captures to some degree the dynamism of his preaching voice. It calls his hearers to a new sense of dignity rooted in God's love as revealed in the election of lowly shepherds to worship the Christ child. Like Jesus' mother, the peasant woman Mary of Nazareth and Jesus' birth as her Galilean son, the shepherds represent one of the core Gospel dynamics: "What human beings reject, God chooses as God's very own."* *

The shepherds, alone with their animals and despised by local society, heard the news: "Today the Savior has been born.... Glory to God in heaven, and on earth, peace to those whom God loves so much" (see Luke 2:11–14). When they arrived at the indicated site and found the sign — the child in the manger — they experienced what the angels had proclaimed: that innermost peace that comes with the experience of being loved. At that moment the shepherds experienced the core of salvation and liberation: No matter what the world thinks of you, you are loved by God.

In the experience of being loved, one becomes capable of loving. Being loved with no conditions attached or questions asked is the radical beginning of a new life. Experiencing love is the beginning of the new life of love. This love dispels fear, loneliness, confusion, hardness, and sadness, and replaces them with tranquility, fellowship, joy, and peace. The world around one does not change immediately, but one changes immediately in relation to the entire world. Truly, peace on earth — the deepest human peace of all — comes to all who today experience how much they are loved by God. Open your hearts wide that you, too, may experience this fascinating and unlimited love that God has for you and for every human being, especially those whom the world does not love.

God reaches out in a very special and concrete way to reassure those whom the world does not love that he loves them

---

*Elizondo, *Galilean Journey,* 91.

most of all! God certainly loves all people, but he loves in a unique way those whom the world despises. For in loving them in a special way God denounces the lie of the world which makes some persons appear to be undignified, unworthy, and unlovable. It is this real experience of love that begins the transformation of everything else.

By now, you are probably saying that all this is fine, but such thoughts merely serve to give people a good feeling without in any way changing the disastrous situations of inequality and oppression that exist both in our neighborhoods and around the world.

Not so! The beginning of liberation is the image of ourselves that we experience within the deepest recess of our hearts. As long as we are convinced that we are inferior and worthless, we will act that way. We will be docile to our masters and subservient to our natural superiors, for it will appear that there is no other way to be. In such cases, fatalism is the only way to survive.

The realization that one has self-worth, fundamental dignity, radical equality, and love is the innermost and deepest beginning of liberation. It certainly does not stop there. But, on the other hand, there is no other authentic beginning. To the degree that we experience ourselves as human beings worthy of respect, to that degree we will experience a new power within us that is stronger and more persevering than any human power: the power of the Spirit of God within us. It is this Spirit that will lead us to shout out from our hearts, "Abba!" And when we have truly experienced that we can thus address God, we likewise become aware of the fundamental equality of all human beings.

This experience is the beginning of the pilgrimage. It makes us free so that we might now struggle to become free, it frees us from the internal enslavement of poor self-image so as to be free to struggle to destroy the exterior obstacles to freedom, dignity, equality, and partnership. The inner experience of fundamental self-worth liberates us to begin the struggle.

The core message of Christmas is that we are of fundamental worth and that we are so much loved by God that he became one of us. In Jesus, God becomes one of us. No matter how inferior or incapable you feel, God wants you, loves you, chooses you, and calls you for a specific mission in this world. You can never be alone, for God is with you and with us: *Emmanuel.*

Thus we can truly cry out from the depth of our hearts, "Joy to the World, the Savior's come!"

— "A Child in a Manger," 68–70

VAMOS PASTORES

For those who have often experienced the pain of being unwanted and denounced, devotions that reinforce identity as children of God and belonging to the household of God are graced pronouncements of saving truth. A number of Mexican American devotions to Christ embody this good news, such as the posadas, where the pilgrims Mary and Joseph are rebuffed at Bethlehem yet are still holy ones of God. Far from seeing them as mere folklore or the piety of the uneducated, Virgilio's writings illuminate the depth of such spiritual practices, as evident in the following meditation that begins with his reflections on a popular Christmas song about the shepherds.

One of the most beautiful and moving songs of the Mexican Christmas tradition is "Vamos Pastores Vamos," which celebrates the excitement of the shepherds going to Bethlehem to see the child who radiates the glory of heaven. It is a very festive song, sometimes even accompanied by dances as the shepherds approach the child in the crib. This song is very close to many of the people, especially since many of them are *campesinos,* often afraid of false offers of help and assistance. So many times offers of help turn out to be mere tricks to rob them. This night, they hear the call that, far from being afraid, they should be rejoicing, since a true savior has been born unto them.

The angels proclaimed to the shepherds: "Do not be afraid; for behold, I proclaim to you good news of great joy that will be for all the people. For today in the city of David a Savior has been born for you who is Messiah and Lord. And this will be a sign for you: you will find an infant wrapped in swaddling clothes and lying in a manger" (Luke 2:10–12).

It is amazing how easy it is for those who are not distracted by the glamour and the shining lights of pomp, commercials, and wealth to see the presence of God in the simple and the ordinary. I have often experienced this among parents and families whose faces radiate with divine joy when holding their own baby or the baby of one of their neighbors in their arms. There is no doubt in their minds that this baby is of God and that its purity and innocence reveal the very beauty of God. They need no rational, philosophical, theological, or ideological proof to establish the divine-like status of this baby. They have no doubts that this baby reflects the very beauty and image of God. I have become especially aware of this in baptisms of the poor at San Fernando Cathedral [in San Antonio]. The poor bring their babies to be baptized with such pride that there is no doubt they see in them a reflection of the divine beauty and dignity. As we baptize the babies, camera flashes go off as proud parents, relatives, and friends record this sacred moment. It is as if God was once again opening up the skies and saying about this baby: "You are my beloved Son, with you I am well pleased" (Luke 3:22).

The shepherds had absolutely nothing but their sheep, pastures, and the beauty of the skies. They were the outcasts of their society because they were considered to be cutthroats and impure, and quite probably because of the bad smell of the sheep, which became part of their own body smell. They were definitely not the ones who would be invited into polite society. They were considered impure persons whose word did not count. They did not need to go to a palace or basilica to find God. They did not need any miracles or biblical proofs that a

savior had been born. They discovered the savior in the nakedness of a baby in a crib. Family name, clothes, and social status
do not determine the dignity of a newborn child; rather by its
very birth the child is a revelation of the grandeur and beauty
of God.   —*A God of Incredible Surprises,* 38–39

"BEGINNING IN GALILEE..."

*Early Christians were careful to note that Jesus and his public
ministry both originated in Galilee. One of the first proclama-
tions of the Gospel included Peter's statement that "I take it
you know what has been reported all over Judea about Jesus of
Nazareth, beginning in Galilee..." (Acts 10:37). The following selection underscores what many consider to be Virgilio's
most original insight: Jesus' Galilean origins are a crucial starting point for probing the mystery of the incarnation and the
totality of the Christ event.*

When God became human, healing humanity through his experience as a person who was wounded and hurt in many ways,
God did not become a generic human being, a Roman, a Greek,
or even an elite Judean Jew. He became a marginal, Galilean
Jew, a village craftsman living with his family and neighbors in
a village situated on the periphery of the political, intellectual,
and religious powers of the world. From his childhood visits
to the Temple to his death on the cross, it is evident that Jesus
loved his Jewish religion with its unwavering hope in the God
who saves. He died as a pious Jew reciting the evening prayer of
his people, placing hope and confidence in the God who saves
(Luke 23:46). It is equally true, however, that he does not seem
to have been limited by an overly strict religious interpretation
of the *Sabbat,* and the codes of purity/impurity and exclusion
that seem to have been common in his times. God's love is
greater than any human tradition that tends to limit or even
hide it (Mark 2:27–28).

Jesus became a man at once distant from all power centers of domination and at the crossroads where various peoples encounter one another. Since grace builds upon nature, I wondered if Jesus' Galilean experience could have been a cultural preparation for the new humanity inaugurated by him and promoted by the New Testament, one that would not be limited by blood or ethnicity. In the end, I started to see the vision of Jesus as rooted in, yet transcending, his experiences in Galilee: a vision that could serve as a prototype of the *fronteras* of the world — whether they be nations or neighborhoods — where diverse peoples encounter one another not to fight, humiliate, or exclude one another, but to form new friendships and families in a space where the "impure" and excluded can find new possibilities and inaugurate new beginnings. Jesus the Galilean Jew who interprets his context in light of God's way thus appears as the doorway — the sheep gate — through which all peoples are invited into the new flock, the new humanity.

In becoming a Galilean Jew, a craftsman in an insignificant village, and son of Mary, Jesus becomes one of the rejects and marginalized of society, along with the millions who suffer exclusion, segregation, and rejection simply because of ethnicity or origin. He suffers in his flesh the multiple effects of the victims of the sin of the world. Yet in his baptism he comes out of this oppressive and dehumanizing situation of rejection as the beloved Son of God (Mark 1:11; Matt. 3:17; Luke 3:22), leaving behind the dehumanizing scars of rejection, while still knowing the pain. From here he sets out on his mission to proclaim the kingdom of God wherein all who believe in him will be welcomed, especially those excluded and humiliated by society. He takes a most common, beautiful, and emotional symbol of his people, the "kingdom of God," and proposes an earth-shaking new interpretation: everyone will be welcomed, beginning with the despised and impure of his society (Matt. 21:31). The "rejected one" rejects rejection by living and proclaiming a universal welcome and love for all. He invites all to repent of their feelings and attitudes of inferiority or superiority, of impurity or purity, of belonging or rejection, and to recognize that we are all children of God called to share in the common table, the table of the new family that goes beyond blood or social status. It is in this experience of radical acceptance that new life begins.

One of the unquestioned constants in the life of Jesus was his association with the socially despised outsiders and untouchables. Through contact with him, the lowliest of society recover their sense of God-given dignity, and the excluded experience a new sense of belonging. Jesus was not afraid to touch and associate with the impure and with public sinners, even dining with them. Jesus loved people and was not afraid to share in their joys and sorrows, regardless of what society thought of them. I suspect that in this he scandalized everyone because he refused to be scandalized by anyone. He did not merely proclaim a new understanding of the kingdom, but he lived it out in his practice of joyful table fellowship with everyone. It was this experience of table fellowship, especially with tax collectors and public sinners, that was most meaningful to Jesus' followers and most offensive and scandalous to his opponents.

The response of Jesus to his Galilean context is a key to the salvific understanding of his identity and mission. In choosing the rejected of our sinful world, God reveals the lie of the world; and in welcoming everyone into the reign of God, beginning with the rejected, God demolishes the power of this world's segregating structures and reveals the truth of God's creation. Creation is for everyone, and not exclusively for any one person or human group. No wonder the Temple veil rips apart upon Jesus' death! This rejection of rejection is good news to the downtrodden but threatening to those in control of status and belonging, whose laws and traditions often exclude and disgrace others (Luke 11:46; Matt. 23:4).

— "Jesus the Galilean Jew in Mestizo Theology," 273–75

SAN ANTONIO GALILEAN

Many biblical figures felt unworthy when God called them. Moses responded, "Who am I that I should go to Pharaoh and lead the Israelites out of Egypt?" (Exod. 3:11). Jeremiah said, "I know not how to speak: I am too young" (1:6). In Luke's Gospel, Peter pleads, "Leave me, Lord. I am a sinful man" (5:8). Jesus' Galilean identity and ministry illuminate the biblical pattern of unexpected divine election. The following selection is one of many examples Virgilio presents of this pattern still active today. This is good news for the Galileans of every time and place. It is good news for all of us, however we have undergone rejection in our lives: through the pain of ethnic prejudice, divorce, poverty, illness, abandonment, or any experience of exclusion or ridicule. Jesus is God's response to the ugliness of rejection that disfigures God's beauty in you, in me, in each one of God's human creations.

Often in working with the poor who have been imprisoned for petty mistakes or with those seeking to escape the daily torture of living in misery by getting into drugs, I have discovered that the Jesus of the Gospels becomes a real source of rebirth. Their insights into the Gospel texts are astounding. I remember Jaime, a young ex-drug addict and ex-prisoner from one of the poor barrios in San Antonio who had discovered Jesus while in prison. He came from one of those areas of the world of which you could ask, "Can anything good come from there?" The poor areas of San Antonio were plagued with inadequate schools, no public libraries, overcrowded homes, and a level of poverty that resulted in malnutrition, poor hygienic conditions, and underemployment. The horrible conditions have led many of our young people into drugs just to escape the horrors and hopelessness of daily life.

From the lowest pits of human existence Jaime had risen to the highest peaks through his personal encounter with Jesus. His language was a rich barrio mixture of Spanish and English that would not be acceptable in any school or pulpit. His language was horrible to the linguistic purists, but the substance of his thought was astounding. He was the leader of my youth Bible group, which gathered about a hundred teenagers every Wednesday night to pray and listen to the Word of God. Jaime would explain the Scriptures to them in language none of us would dare to use in the pulpit or classroom, but a language which made the Jesus message come alive for the teenagers. He had only completed eighth grade and never studied Scriptures or much of anything else, yet his insights into the meaning of the text were fascinating. I was constantly amazed at his wisdom. Once I brought in a biblical scholar to listen to him. We both agreed that this young man truly had the grace of interpretation. He had no formal studies, but he expressed insights richer and far beyond many of those found in the finest of biblical commentaries.

In many ways, Jaime was like a modern Galilean Jesus. His own experience of deprivation, marginalization, and suffering gave him insights into the saving and liberating dynamics of Jesus that many of us had not suspected. He was considered nothing by the world. I am sure that because of his past record I would not have been able to get him into the seminary even if he had wanted to be a priest. Yet I am convinced he was anointed by God to bring young people to Christ. They flocked to him in great numbers, and some even claimed that they had been healed through his prayers. Was he performing miracles? For some, there was no doubt. Yet upon seeing and hearing Jaime, others wondered how I could allow such a "trashy" and "uncultivated" man to lead our youth prayer group and no doubt asked in their hearts: "Can anything good come from the barrios of the poor?" — *A God of Incredible Surprises,* 47–48

TABLE FELLOWSHIP

Jesus' contemporaries tried to understand him and his Galilean ministry within the categories of the day: teacher, prophet, rabbi. In the end his followers concluded that other religious leaders paled in comparison to their Master. He was, as Virgilio has so beautifully expressed it, a rejected Galilean who rejected the world's rejection and proclaimed to the rejected of Galilee the good news of God's universal love. His preaching uplifted the lowly with this saving message. His healings and exorcisms alleviated their suffering, eradicated their plight as outcasts, and restored them to the life of community. As the following selection shows, his table fellowship — the most characteristic aspect of Jesus' ministry before, during, and after his passion and resurrection — enacted his good news among all, the pious as well as those despised as sinners.

Joyful table fellowship with anyone and everyone was one of the most regular aspects of the life and ministry of Jesus, and it was without doubt what caused the greatest furor. John the Baptist and his disciples, like the Pharisees and other holiness groups, fasted while Jesus and his followers feasted! One was the way of penance; the other was the way of fiesta. "And they said to him, 'The disciples of John fast often and offer prayers, and the disciples of the Pharisees do the same; but yours eat and drink'" (Luke 5:33). I often wonder how many of our Christian church services today truly resemble this joyful table fellowship of Jesus.

There is an irony in this all-inclusive community that Jesus is initiating. It is scandalous and dangerous to those who have held the monopoly on status and belonging, to the custodians of the status quo. Their rules and customs are de-authorized and rendered ineffective. Everyone is now invited, but not everyone will come. Many will stay away not because they are not invited but precisely because now everyone is invited. Those who have had the privileged invitations to the places of worldly prestige and honor will not want to mix and rub shoulders with the insignificant and "worthless" people of society. They will indeed be invited, as in the parable of the great wedding feast of Luke 14:15–24, but they will offer silly excuses why they cannot come. Thus, because Jesus rejects exclusion, some will choose to exclude themselves!....

The greatest miracle of Jesus — one that has not been looked upon as a miracle and yet it is the one that the very first Christians remembered with such fondness that they continued practicing it daily — was his joy of radically inclusive table fellowship. In his company, strangers became friends and foreigners became blood family. Jesus loved to have a good time with close friends and with anyone and everyone. This was not a one-time affair. In fact, it was so regular and ordinary during the earthly life of Jesus that the early Christians who wanted to follow his way made it the greatest characteristic of their own new life. This is what attracted so many to join the new group. It was not just new teachings about God, but the new experience of a unifying God who could bring all people together in a festive and loving way.

Jesus brings his earthly ministry to completion in a very similar way in which he started: a festive meal with his friends. What has come to be known as the last supper was precisely that, the last of what had been most regular in the life of Jesus. In this final festive meal, Jesus gives us the connection between the ongoing sacrifice of his life for the sake of the inclusion of others to the final sacrifice which will be demanded of him by those who opposed this radical desegregation of humanity in the name of the God who is Father of all. Yet even when they got rid of him on the cross, they could not put a stop to the new practice of festive-inclusive meals that in turn gave rise to new social relations and concerns for the welfare of one another.

After the resurrection, Jesus gives instructions to his disciples that they are to go to Galilee, and there they will see him. They did so, and one early morning after they had been fishing all night and catching nothing, Jesus appeared and told them to cast the net on the other side, very much like at Cana, telling them to do something that humanly speaking did not make sense. But they did it and caught a huge amount, so huge that their nets were on the point of breaking. While they were doing this, Jesus was on the shore nearby preparing breakfast for them, an early morning barbecue for his friends. In the context of this simple yet festive meal with his followers, Jesus asks Peter: "Do you love me?" (John 21:15). He did not ask Peter: "Do you now understand everything I have taught you?" or "Will you now be strong enough not to deny me again?" or "Do you think you have the proper qualities to lead my followers?" He simply asks him in the very context of table fellowship, "Do you love me?" Peter answers in the affirmative and is thus commissioned to lead the flock. Yes, it is not through authoritarian power that we are to lead but through loving service, creating spaces in the midst of empires wherein everyone will be welcomed, recognized, accepted, and valued. Like Jesus, we will scandalize those who defend exclusive domains that exclude others under various excuses and practical reasons. But we, following in the steps of our Master, will continue to find new ways of building an alternative world wherein nobody will be excluded and we will continue beginning where Jesus began: in the festive meals to which all are invited.

—*A God of Incredible Surprises*, 90, 94–95

CRUCIFIXION

Virgilio insists there is an intrinsic link between the way Jesus chose to live and the way he died. He avows that Jesus' Galilean ministry of proclaiming God's love in word and deed, especially to the unwanted, led him to confront the system that labeled Galileans and others as impure and diminished their dignity as children of God. The crucifixion cannot be fully understood apart from Jesus' struggle against the injustice that dehumanizes marginal people such as Galileans. Jesus' sacrificial death reveals another core dynamic of the Gospel: "It is not sufficient to do good and avoid evil: the disciple must do good and struggle against evil."*

---

*Elizondo, *Galilean Journey*, 72.

His detractors called him a blasphemer and a troublemaker; questioned by his family, he was eventually "handed over" to the Romans, who condemned him to crucifixion. Thus Jesus must confront the structures that legitimize the unjust ways of his sinful world that hide and pervert the truth of God. He must go to Jerusalem where the Jewish aristocratic elite collaborated with the Roman authorities in the domination and exploitation of their own people. He goes to confront, not with violence, military might, or armed revolution, but as the suffering servant who confronts only with the power of truth in the service of love. He came to break the spiral of violence, and even if the cost was the cross, he would triumph through the power of unlimited love. While it is never easy, Jesus shows us that we must confront the sin structured so deeply within our own ways of life that we often take it as natural, sometimes even sacred, truth!

When we see through the seeming tragedy of Golgotha and discover that sin, both structural and personal, was the real cause of this drama, we realize that blaming the Jewish people or even their first-century elites can lead us to ignore the role of our own sinfulness today, which crucifies not one, but many people. Only when we can see that it was the twisted logic of power and unjust social structures that demanded the crucifixion of Jesus (John 11:50; Mark 14:1b; Luke 22:2, 26:4) will we begin to unveil the same absurdities that continue to demand the crucifixions of prophets and the innocent victims of every type. Blaming the Jewish people or even their leaders is an easy way to mask our own unjust social arrangements (our idols) and to ignore their consequences.

Misuse of Scripture is not uncommon. Many in Europe marginalized and persecuted our Jewish brothers and sisters out of a warped reading of the Gospel. Many in the Americas used Scripture to justify the enslavement of Africans, the exploitation of the Amerindians through the *encomienda* system as an aspect of evangelization, and the elimination of the natives as God's will. Some in the United States today justify persecuting and imprisoning poor, defenseless, undocumented immigrants through a superficial reading of Romans 13 on obedience to civil authority. This perversion of the Gospel must be denounced. Jesus is the prophet who remains faithful to the poor and confronts injustice with the power of love in the service of truth. He witnesses to the truth that love unites all in a new humanity; knowing it would cost him his life, he did not remain silent.

In rejecting Jesus, those invested in the sinful structures he sought to change decided he must be eliminated; they even stirred up the people to demand his crucifixion. The one who rejects rejection is violently rejected by the leaders and people of a disordered world. With his death on the cross, it remains to be seen whose way is true. Yet in raising him from the dead, God identifies the way of Jesus as his own, confirming that his announcement of God's kingdom of love, reconciliation, and compassion will always be a challenge to the unjust persons and structures of the world. The power of God's loving truth will triumph over the powers of death and the forces of evil, no matter how righteous and sacred they might appear to be.

— "Jesus the Galilean Jew in Mestizo Theology," 275–77

LAST WORDS

The siete palabras *or seven last words of Christ is a popular Good Friday tradition among Mexican Americans and other Latinos. It entails a solemn proclamation of the seven statements Jesus makes from the cross in the four Gospels, each proclamation accompanied with a sermon or some sort of meditation. This tradition draws on Latinos' deep reverence for those who are dying and on their tendency to cherish the final words their loved ones utter. The following brief meditation on the* siete palabras *appeared in an editorial of a San Antonio newspaper when Virgilio served as rector of San Fernando Cathedral.*

There are so many things I would like to say about Jesus of Nazareth, whose life and death have given new life to millions across the ages and across the planet, but I will limit myself to a brief reflection on his final gift to us — his last words from the cross, which are the everlasting words of life.

As he hangs on the cross at San Antonio's Main Plaza at noon Friday, we will once again hear those simple but profound words of a dying man whose love for us is so great that even in being nailed to the cross he struggles to free us, who even in dying struggles to bring us to life in its fullness.

"Father, forgive them for they know not what they do."
—Luke 23:34

From the throne of his cathedral, Jesus proclaimed the most beautiful, powerful word of life: forgive. In a world poisoned and torn by violence, vengeance, betrayals, abandonments, insults, and indifference, forgiveness is the only way to inner freedom and peace. It liberates and restores life.

Without forgiveness, life is worse than death, and death is eternal torment. Jesus was betrayed, abused, and abandoned. Yet he lived to forgive. For only in forgiveness is even death dissolved into life everlasting and pain transformed into unending joy.

"Today you shall be with me in Paradise." — Luke 23:43

Is there one of us who has not failed in some way? Acting as if no wrong had been done is as great a sickness as constantly accusing oneself. But unquestioned trust in the one who dies for us rehabilitates anyone. As always, Jesus has the way to inner healing: Simply admit your guilt, trust in him, and God will do the rest. "Today you shall be with me in Paradise."

"Woman, behold your son. . . . Behold your mother."
—John 19:26–27

No one should ever be left alone or unattended. To be really alive, we need to love and be loved. Not even death should separate us from those we love, from those who in life have given us life.

Jesus' physical agony on the cross is transcended by his compassion, his tender care for those around him. Only in caring for others does our own suffering become submerged in the peace of eternal life — not the life of the hereafter, but the beginning of eternal life, which is found in today's bonds of loving concern and care.

"My God, my God, why have you abandoned me?"
— Matthew 27:46

What an incredible love Jesus showed for all of us! There is no greater love than to share in the deepest agony of the beloved. Jesus, in his own body and spirit, shared our excruciating pains of embarrassment, shame, failure, alienation, loneliness, and distress.

I need not ever fear or despair. For I know that the Son of God is with me to give me a hope beyond all human hope: that God will triumph in me. In the abandonment of Jesus, I am rescued from my own abandonment, for God is always with me, no matter what.

"I thirst." — John 19:28

Jesus was condemned by his people and abandoned by his friends. The thousands who wanted to make him king demanded his death. When all goes well, we have plenty of friends and followers. When it doesn't, we are quickly maligned and deserted.

The deepest thirst of the human spirit is for understanding, acceptance, and companionship. Only we can offer this drink of life to a parched human heart.

"It is finished!" — John 19:30

This is an affirmation of triumph, not defeat. Jesus remained faithful to God's project for humanity: to love others no matter the cost, no matter the response, "that all might be one."

Death is not the end of life, but merely the completion of life's project, which, as with every great piece of art, lives forever.

"Father, into your hands I commend my spirit."
                                                    —Luke 23:46

What a beautiful way to depart this world — with complete confidence in the God of life.

After entrusting my life and my destiny to God, I, like Jesus, can enter into the peace and bliss of knowing that I have done my best in living God's will, and God asks nothing more.

For God wills that I live life to the fullest, and in seeking to do God's will, I come to the fullness of life both here and in eternity.   — "Jesus' Dying Words Give Us Life"

BREAKING THE CYCLE OF VENGEANCE

Virgilio presents Jesus — the rejected, abandoned, and crucified Galilean — as the courageous reconciler who refused to lash out at his offenders. In him we find the way to rupture the spirit of vengeance that plagues wounded humanity.

God's saving entry into human affairs seeks to break with the way of victimization and violence. God wants a good life for all, but not at the cost of any. The God of the Bible does not want victims! God stops Abraham from sacrificing his son, leads the slaves out of Egypt, and will go to the point of allowing his own Son to offer his life in sacrifice rather than victimizing anyone. These are privileged moments of the biblical experience of God.

The Bible begins by affirming the origins of all human beings; we are all descendants of Adam and Eve, who were created in the image and likeness of God and are therefore of intrinsic beauty and infinite worth. But Adam and Eve went their own way, Cain killed his brother, and all generations will learn and develop the ways of the first ones! God's creation has gone sour! This corruption has become so ingrained in the inner depths of the human spirit — both collective and personal — that even God will not easily cleanse his people of their false ideas about life: God takes the people out of Egypt much more easily than he can take Egypt's way of life out of their minds and hearts.

But God, being the loving parent that God is, will not let creation destroy itself. The main focus of the entire biblical adventure is God's identification with and concern for the oppressed victims. In the Exodus, God hears the cries of God's people, sees their suffering, and determines to come and save them; during the glorious days of the Israelite kingdom, God speaks through the prophets in favor of the widows, the orphans, and the foreigners who are being exploited by their very own! In the exile God comforts the people living in a foreign land and offers them hope. In the poems of the suffering servant in the prophet Isaiah, it is not God who afflicts the servant, but God who speaks through him, through the excluded and despised other, to offer hope to all others. God does not will victimization, but uses the victims to bring salvation to all — victims and victimizers alike. It is the victim who is God's instrument of ultimate triumph! But it is evident from the failures of the Old Testament drama that it was not enough for God to enter into solidarity with the victims of society as a concerned outsider.

Human beings are of such infinite worth that God sends his Son to enter into ultimate solidarity with the victims of this world by himself being born a victim — Jewish (world's outcasts), Galilean (despised by fellow Jews), and son of Mary (of questionable parentage), Jesus lived a constantly victimized life and died a victim. The core of the revelation of Jesus is that he refuses to accept the image of a good and successful human being from any of the victimizers of his society — religious, spiritual, economic, political, or revolutionary. Unlike us, he will never seek to follow the way of his victimizers; he refuses to idealize their goals or try to become like them in any way. In this way, he demonstrates complete freedom, even though tempted, from the repetitive cycles of violence and victimization and ends up disappointing everyone — even his disciples. He was altogether "too much" (Matt. 13:57).

Jesus introduces a radically refreshing and liberating image of the authentic human being: I am who am! It does not matter who my parents are, my social or economic status, my nationality or race. If God, the all-powerful creator and absolute master of the universe, is my father, then no humanly created category of identification can erase or hide my ultimate and only truly real identity. My ultimate status and identity come not from human beings, but from God.

Because I am, I am of infinite worth, unique beauty, and sacred dignity! This was the supreme truth that the world's cultures of dominance and victimization could not stand to have revealed, for it demolished and demonstrated clearly the fallacy of their rationalizations and justifications that legitimized their power claims over weak and defenseless human beings.

This revelation makes of Jesus an intolerable rabble-rouser — one who subverts the masses. This is why he must die, for he is disturbing the very foundations — sociological, cultural, and religious — of human groups based on dehumanizing differentiation and segregation. Jesus was born a victim, was a victim of false accusations throughout his life, and died a victim condemned by false accusations. Yet he refused to give in to victimization! He offered salvation to all — victims and victimizers alike — because he refused to imitate the humanly accepted patterns of victimization and invited us to do the same! Free to be without having to destroy anyone! That is the ultimate liberation.

It is in the cross that the ultimate victimization of the weak is revealed: "They all cried out, 'Crucify him'" (Luke 23:21), while the ultimate loving and saving power of God is equally revealed through the crucified victim: "Father, forgive them, for they know not what they do" (Luke 23:34). Incredible as it sounds, the evil of human beings allows the ultimate glory of God to become manifest and, in so doing, the destructive cycle of victimization has finally been broken.

God was supremely revealed and experienced at one of the most unreligious and least spiritual moments of human history: the cruel and bloody execution of an innocent victim. The nakedness of the victim Jesus dying on the cross revealed in its most stark form the unlimited love and compassion of God who allows his Son to be sacrificed rather than allowing others to be victimized. Through this love, violence and destructiveness have been conquered without destroying the very persons who have sought to perpetuate victimization.

— "Evil and the Experience of God," 36–38

WAY OF THE CROSS

Mexican American prayer traditions, especially their fervent devotion to the passion of Christ and his sorrowful mother, mediate the belief that persevering through struggles, suffering, and even death is the way of Christ and the saints. The following passage relates the redemptive meaning of the cross in a sinful and violent world, as well as the demand for conversion of heart that Christ's way of the cross places on us. It comes from Virgilio's edited book The Way of the Cross of the Americas, *a series of meditations that explore Jesus' passion against the backdrop of the five hundredth anniversary of the conquest of the Americas.*

One of the most traditional and popular devotions in the Christian world is the Stations of the Cross. Ancient tradition tells us that after Jesus' Ascension Mary was the first to retrace the steps of her son's passion and death. The church has never required dogmatic assent to this belief; but every generation of Christians, driven by some instinct of faith, has tried to retrace the steps of Jesus to Calvary, discovering that he continues to journey with us in our own passion and way of the cross. In him our own Calvary takes on new meaning.

I have retraced the way of the cross since childhood. In my [former] parish church in Texas, San Fernando Cathedral, it continues to be the most popular devotion. And each year in my present city, San Antonio, merchants stop doing business at noon on Good Friday so that everyone may follow the way of the cross. The world joins with the Holy Father when he takes up the cross in the evening of Good Friday and leads us all in this traditional devotion.

As I make the way of the cross each year, I note that the suffering has not been erased, loneliness continues, and the betrayal and abandonment of friends breaks my heart. The lashes of the whip still go on, the crown of thorns continues to make me bleed, the unjust condemnations make me wonder about divine justice, and the death of innocent victims causes me to cry out: "Lord, why have you forsaken us?" Nothing has changed and there does not seem to be much point in continuing to meditate on the Way of the Cross.

It may indeed seem that nothing changes, indeed that the world is getting worse. But what *is* changing is my heart. Each time we make the Stations of the Cross we discover more of the drama in the great battle to end all battles: the clash between God's limitless love and our own love — conditioned, limited, and even perverted by material riches and the social demands of this world. But what slow learners we are! Through the centuries we Christians have preferred to destroy with wars and conquests rather than to build new societies of harmony, mutual help, honest work, reconciliation, and love. War has been far more attractive than peace, and the conquerors have appeared far more attractive than the confessors, prophets, and martyrs.

The history of the Christian world, sad to say, has been a history of every possible kind of warfare. In this century we have witnessed two world wars with Christians killing Christians. The atomic bomb came from a Christian country. Christian countries initiate the massive arms sales to peoples and nations in need of food and medicine. And Christian countries produce the most powerful armies in the world. It seems that the greatness of a human being is measured by his ability to kill other human beings, and our heroes are the military leaders who kill in cold blood anyone who seems to be an enemy.

We are scandalized by the human sacrifices of our Aztec ancestors, but we sacrifice many more people on the altars of modern technological warfare without batting an eye. How many innocent people have died in the wars of Central America or on the streets of Brazil? How many innocent people were killed or buried alive in the war against Iraq? And where are we Christians? What do we have to say about all this?

We continue to glorify the destructive forces of this world. We say our cultures are in good order and committed to equality, justice, brotherhood, science, technology, progress, and human development; but the masses continue to suffer exploitation and die of hunger. We call ourselves civilized and our victims uncivilized. We worry about the disappearance of the Amazon rain forest but we do not worry about the disappearance of its human inhabitants. We debate ecological issues, but we close our eyes to the millions of poor people who live, work, and die in lands contaminated by our radioactive waste.

In the way of the cross the most incomprehensible injustices experienced in my lifetime take on liberative and redemptive significance. Far from justifying the injustices of our world, the way of the cross from Jesus' day to our day continues to rip away the sacred curtain around what is deemed good, attractive, just, and even holy in this world. It shows those things for what they really are: ugly, rotten, even Satanic. At the same time it reveals the ones who are truly God's good and holy ones: those who freely love to the point of giving their lives for others, even for people who betray, abandon, and condemn them to death. They are unjustly condemned to death by those who feel threatened by God's limitless love. The way of the cross continues to reveal the persistent malice of a world dominated by sin and the inexhaustible love of a God who seeks to save us in spite of ourselves.

The Americas have been a font of hope and new life for many people around the world in the last five hundred years. We hope and pray that the God of life will resurrect those other people for whom the Americas have largely been a cross and Calvary. We pray that God may destroy in us everything that leads to the suffering and death of others, turning us into agents of new life rather than of death.   — *Way of the Cross*, xii–xiv

RESURRECTION AND PENTECOST

The following passage advances Virgilio's explication of the Galilean Jesus beyond the agony of the cross. In his encounters with first his women disciples of Galilee, then the men, and ultimately with believers down to us, our risen Lord engenders hope and transformation through the power of his resurrection. He sends his Holy Spirit to embolden his followers in their faith. The church is born at Pentecost in the Spirit-filled preaching of his Galilean disciples. It is born anew whenever the world's Galileans announce the vastness of God's love revealed in Christ, confront structures of oppressive divisiveness, and enact the universal fellowship of God's new creation. The resurrection and Pentecost reveal the foundational dynamic of the Gospels: "no human power can prevail against the power of [God's] unlimited love." *

Encounter with the risen Lord transforms those who experience him. Recalling how meeting with certain persons has deeply affected us and might have changed us can help us somewhat to understand what happened in the encounter between the apostles and the risen Lord. But we can never fully understand

---

*Elizondo, *Galilean Journey*, 115.

it: no human encounter can be fully adequate to the encounter with the risen Lord.

This transforming encounter was an illuminating experience as well, for through it the apostles begin to see the entire way of Jesus in a new light — that is, in the light of a deepened faith. Those who had followed Jesus from Galilee with some degree of faith now recognize him in a different way, and in this recognition of him as the risen Lord they are themselves transformed and illuminated. Those who encounter the risen Lord are created anew from within, with the result that they relate in a new way to God, to other persons, institutions, and the world. It is a totally new way of situating themselves within the human condition.

Paul cites as a "proof" of "our status as adopted sons" the experience of God's sending into their hearts "the spirit of his Son which cries out 'Abba'" (Gal. 4:6). It is through the experience of the risen Lord that they were reborn and knew themselves to be sons and daughters of the one Father. This transforming experience was the beginning of new life — the beginning of the new creation.

It was in the power of the risen Lord that the early community of faith retraced the meaning of the liberating way of Jesus from Nazareth to Jerusalem and interiorized the meaning of his risen presence. This took place in various ways but especially through the ongoing celebration of what had been so characteristic of Jesus: the joy of table fellowship with all persons, especially the most rejected and marginalized of society. They now begin to relate in a new way to their fellow human beings. There is not a new law to this effect, but a new celebration. The life of unlimited love that will refuse to be limited or enslaved by the letter of any law — written laws, customs, or traditions — now begins to be lived by the followers of the resurrected Lord. True life and happiness comes from loving as God himself loves, which means the rejection of any humanly made obstacles that limit our ability to love. Christian love means to be perfect as the heavenly Father is perfect: he makes his sun rise on the evil and the good and sends rain on the just and the unjust (Matt. 5:43–48).

It is from within the perspective of their new existence and new understanding that the followers of Jesus now begin to look back into their memory of the earthly Jesus in attempting to answer the all-important question: Who was Jesus of Nazareth? The experience of resurrection is both an original and an originating experience, for it gives rise to the beginning of the process that brings us into the inner knowledge of the whole inner mystery of Christ — from the incarnation to the resurrection and exaltation.

The community of faith was then and is today the starting point of all Christological reflection. Because we believe, because we experience him in faith, because we have been transformed through personal encounter with the risen Lord, we seek to articulate our understanding of this person in whom we have been reborn. The existential believing community, historically and culturally situated, is the starting point of Christian reflection. Any other starting point would tend to be mere theory, speculation, or ideology rather than authentic reflection of the intellect seeking a deeper understanding of the faith — not an abstract faith, but the real, living, dynamic, imperfect, and culturally conditioned life of the church.

In the light of the resurrection, the liberating meaning and necessity of the Galilee-Jerusalem struggle begins to emerge. From the final fulfillment, we go back to the starting point so that we too may walk the same way following the salvific way of Jesus. The resurrected Lord himself sends his followers to the starting point: "Go carry the news to my brothers that they are to go to Galilee, where they will see me" (Matt. 28:10). Without the resurrection, the Galilee-to-Jerusalem process would simply perpetuate the cycle of violence and there would seem to be no way out. But without the Galilee-to-Jerusalem process, the resurrection experience would easily be reduced to a mere "good feeling" with the Lord, which we could even forget.

The cross without the resurrection would be without value and only a curse, but the resurrection without the way of the cross would be a pure utopian dream or illusion. It is only in the whole mystery of Jesus Christ that the mystery of humanity is truly revealed. It is only in the whole mystery of Christ that the necessary process for the liberation of humanity will take place and be celebrated.

The resurrection is the definitive breakthrough of God that penetrates and transcends the human dilemma in which violence only begets greater violence and new forms of violence. We struggle for liberation only to discover ourselves enslaved in new ways. Humanly speaking, there appears to be no way out. In the way of Jesus we discover that violence can only be eliminated through the power of unconditioned and unlimited love.

This love can be found only in unconditional surrender to the love of God-Abba. Only when we experience the absorbing love of God in Jesus — only when we have been grasped by Christ (Phil. 3:12) — can we become lovers in his style. Only when we experience his love can we begin to love as he does (Phil. 2:7–11; John 4). Only then can we begin to move from the violence that we resort to for the sake of self-preservation (of self, institutions, or groups) to the freely accepted violence that we must endure for the life and liberation of others: "There is no greater love than this: to lay down one's life for one's friends" (John 15:13).

> When the day of Pentecost came it found them gathered in one place. Suddenly...there came a noise like a strong, driving wind.... Tongues as of fire appeared, which parted and came to rest on each of them. All were filled with the Holy Spirit. They began to express themselves in foreign tongues.... Staying in Jerusalem at the time were devout Jews of every nation.... They were much confused because each one heard these men speaking his own language.... Peter stood up with the Eleven, raised his voice, and addressed them.... "Jesus the Nazarene was

a man whom God sent to you. . . . He was delivered up. . . .
You even made use of pagans to crucify and kill him. God
freed him from death's bitter pangs, however, and raised
him up again. . . . You must reform and be baptized . . . in
the name of Jesus Christ" (Acts 2:1–38).

In his account of the new Pentecost — the harvest feast that
commemorated the giving of the covenant on Sinai — Luke
uses images reminiscent of the first Sinai ("tongues as of fire,"
cf. Exod. 19:18). But those present are not given a new *law,*
inscribed on *stone;* they are given the *Spirit* who will re-create
them *from within.*

The Spirit ushers in the new creation — a people united in
their experience of being accepted and loved by God freed from
the enslaving tendencies of "the world." The Spirit-filled person will live in love, joy, peace, tolerance, goodness, generosity,
fidelity, simplicity, and self-control (Gal. 5:22–24).

In presenting the history of the early church in Acts, Luke
records the history of the power and works of the Holy Spirit.
Nor is it presented simply as a piece of history, but in order to
give the church of the future a model to live by.

The prophecies of Jeremiah (31:31–34) and Ezekiel (36:25–
29) about the new law "within" and the "new person" are now
being fulfilled. The new people of God is about to take possession of its promised land, which is all humanity, all ethnic
groupings, all nations. No frontiers can deflect this movement.
And the way in which the new people will take possession is
very important: not by imposition or conquest, but by the gift of
the re-creating Spirit, bringing to perfection — not destroying —
what is already there.

There will be a new language, truly universal: the language of
agape. It is the language of selflessness in the service of others,
the language of the radical acceptance and love of the other as
other. It is a language of the heart, communicating directly with
others regardless of human differences.

The Spirit begins the work of transformation with Jesus' apostles. Before, they had been ignorant, difficult to understand, somewhat exclusivist in their thinking, concerned about getting to the power positions, often ready to resort to violence, and quick to run out at moments of difficulty. But now they appear totally different. Peter, who had even denied the Lord, speaks boldly before the crowds and everyone understands him. Peter and the other disciples were probably just as shocked and surprised as the rest of the crowd, for the Galileans, who had not been understood by anyone, are now understood by everyone! But even more than that, hotheaded Peter does not call for mobilization of the masses against anyone; he invites all to repentance and acceptance of God's forgiveness.

Society's rejects — now reborn of God — begin to invite everyone to the new way that has been shown to them. All are invited, but they must open their hearts to the influence of the Spirit in order to be converted to the new way of life preached and inaugurated by Jesus.

The reality of the message of Jesus became embodied in the members of the primitive church. It was sealed in their hearts and engraved on their minds. It was not arguments but their new way of life that attested to the truth of their radical newness. They had a new vision, a new code of ethics, a new joy, a new fellowship, a new strength, a new self-confidence, and a new courage that totally surpassed anything the world had ever known before. Humanly speaking, they simply did not make sense, but they had no doubts whatsoever about their new life and new identity. Material possessions would no longer be a divisive factor; they were freely given to the church to be distributed among the needy. They discovered the joy of giving and sharing, and the happiness of being able to be themselves without the need for masks or artificiality. Through the power of the Spirit, they all experienced a new interpersonal communion. And from the very beginning they understood and accepted with certainty the universal dimension of their new life: it was not just for them, but for all the peoples of the world....

Immediately before the ascension, the risen Lord had given his disciples his final instructions: "You will receive power when the Holy Spirit comes upon you; then you are to be my witnesses...even to the ends of the earth" (Acts 1:8).

The mandate is very specific. They are to go forth and proclaim with their lives and their words what they have personally experienced. They are the ones who have both seen and heard Jesus — from his baptism to his ascension. The totality of the way of Jesus, which they have taken part in, they are now to live out and transmit "to the ends of the earth." It is not of their own accord or through their own wisdom and power that they will act and speak; the Spirit will come upon them and lead them not only to the geographical ends of the earth, but to all the strata of human life and human society.

The early spread of Christianity, especially in the view of the multiple crossings of religious, cultural, and political boundaries — "polarizations" — that it entailed, was nothing less than miraculous. The first disciples were Galileans. As we have already brought out, they were usually viewed as inferior — "ignoramuses, clods" — by their compatriots. Furthermore, some Galileans, especially among the Zealots, were quite exclusivist in their thinking — "no outsiders allowed in!" The rejected, ghetto-minded, "provincial" Galileans are the ones chosen to go out and invite *everyone* to the way of Jesus! How ridiculous it must have seemed to everyone, including the Galileans themselves.

The composition of the first lists of converts to the way of Jesus shows how "successful" God was with the "unlikely" witness of the Galileans: there were Jewish priests (Acts 6:7), Samaritans (8:4–25), Ethiopians (9:26–40), and a Roman centurion (10:1–48). The new way was for everyone; no one was excluded because of race, color, nationality, class, or culture. What mattered was one's openness to belief in Jesus.

The Spirit guided the community to continue what had been so original and meaningful in the earthly life of Jesus: table fellowship with all. The joyous table fellowship was an antic-ipation of the greater joy yet to be expected — the fullness of the kingdom: "I tell you, many will come from east and west and sit at table with Abraham, Isaac, and Jacob in the kingdom of heaven" (Matt. 8:11). It was the celebration of the universal human family begun but not completed. The various members, without ceasing to be who they were, none-theless saw themselves and others in such a way that they could come together as scribes, tax collectors, priests, Pharisees, Zealots, Romans, Greeks, Samaritans, Ethiopians ... to share at the common table. — *Galilean Journey,* 80–85

3

Guadalupe:
An American Gospel

Guadalupe has to do with the very core of the Gospel
itself. — *Guadalupe: Mother of the New Creation, 134*

*Devotion to Our Lady of Guadalupe has evolved and ex-
panded for nearly five centuries. The Guadalupe basilica on the
hill of Tepeyac in Mexico City is the most visited pilgrimage
site on the American continent. After Jesus of Nazareth, her
image is the most reproduced sacred icon in the hemisphere.
She appears among an increasingly diverse array of peoples and
places in North America and beyond: on home altars, T-shirts,
tattoos, murals, parish churches, medals, refrigerator magnets,
wall hangings, and in countless conversations and daily prayers.
She has been long acclaimed as the national symbol of Mexico, and in the 1999 apostolic exhortation* Ecclesia in America
*Pope John Paul II acclaimed her as "an impressive example of a
perfectly inculturated evangelization" of the Gospel and as the
"mother and evangelizer of America" (no. 11), from Tierra del
Fuego to the northernmost reaches of Canada. At the unani-
mous request of the Catholic bishops of the hemisphere, he also
decreed that her feast "be celebrated throughout the continent"
(no. 11). Basilicas and shrines dedicated to her are as far south*

as Santa Fe, Argentina, and as far north as Johnstown, Cape Breton, Nova Scotia.

Widely renowned as one of the foremost writers on Guadalupe, Virgilio acclaims the Guadalupe narrative, image, and devotion as an "American Gospel,"* a tradition deeply rooted both in the soil of the New World and in the Gospel dynamics. The selections in this chapter present highlights from Virgilio's scores of spiritual reflections on Our Lady of Guadalupe. He examines the encounters between Our Lady of Guadalupe and Juan Diego within the context of the clash of civilizations as Spaniards vanquished the indigenous peoples. He unveils evangelical dimensions of the Nican Mopohua, the Nahua account of the Guadalupe apparitions. He explores the meaning of the ever growing fascination with Guadalupe among her numerous children who encounter her maternal love in their daily lives and devotion. He prays that we will all live Guadalupe's call to conversion and unite as her children at the banquet table of her son Jesus Christ.

THE COMMUNION OF TEPEYAC

In the following passage Virgilio presents childhood memories from his first of many pilgrimages to the basilica of Our Lady of Guadalupe in Mexico City. His lifelong devotion to Guadalupe evolved from a family tradition in childhood to a core expression of adult faith to a topic of enduring fascination in his spiritual writings and theological investigations.

When I was six or seven, my father took me on my first pilgrimage to her shrine at Tepeyac. I will never forget it. The trip from San Antonio took three long days of difficult driving through seemingly endless deserts and then over beautiful mountains whose peaks touched the heavens. Driving in and

---

*Elizondo, *Guadalupe: Mother of the New Creation*, 134.

out of the clouds was one of the most exciting adventures I had ever had. It was heavenly, and yet it was so earthy. The tropical fruit we ate on the way was the most exquisite I had ever tasted or have ever tasted since. The closer we got to Mexico City, the slower the clock seemed to move.

I had grown up hearing all kinds of marvelous stories and testimonies about Our Lady of Guadalupe. I felt I already knew her well and couldn't wait to meet her personally. The anticipation grew as we slowly walked down the Avenida de los Misterios leading to the basilica that houses her miraculous image. The long lines of vendors selling flowers, cold drinks, rosaries, tamales, medals, candles, candies, *milagritos,** post cards, and many other items of interest to the pilgrims added to the excitement. The praying and the singing of the people harmonized beautifully with the shouts of the vendors and the noise of the traffic. All were preparing us for the magnificent, mystical encounter that we were gradually approaching.

We finally arrived at the basilica in rhythmic procession with the thousands of others who moved, it seemed, as one collective body. When we entered through the huge doors and into the cool and dark interior (it was very hot outside), it was as if we were all entering together into the common womb of the Americas. As we gradually walked toward the luminous image, she appeared to be coming toward us, as if she were descending to greet each one of us personally. Through the darkness we walked toward the light, the warmth, and the beauty of La Virgen Morena. We could not stop; the crowd simply moved us on. We were never pushed or shoved; we all simply walked in deep mystical union with one another. We were in the rhythmic movement of the universe — indeed, at this moment we were in contact with the very source of life and movement.

I needed no explanation for my experience. I had lived it. In that sacred space, I was part of the communion of earth and

---

*Milagritos: literally "little miracles." Miniature hands, arms, or other limbs presented in thanksgiving or for intercession for the healing of illness or for other needs.

heaven, of present family, ancestors, and generations to come. It became one of the core moments of my life.

— *Guadalupe: Mother of the New Creation,* ix–x

A VIOLENT EVANGELISM

A decade before the 1531 apparitions of Our Lady of Guadalupe, Spanish forces under conquistador Hernán Cortés imposed Spanish rule on Mexico's former Aztec Empire and subjugated the native peoples. In the following selection, Virgilio relates the contradictions of an evangelization process conducted within the context of violence. He notes the worst aspect of the Spanish conquest was not military defeat nor exploitation, as painful as those realities were, but the attempt to destroy the natives' ancestral traditions and worldview, rupturing their sense of their own humanity and leaving them spiritually adrift.

To appreciate the profound meaning of Guadalupe it is important to know the historical setting at the time of the apparition. Suddenly an exterior force, the white men of Europe, intruded on the closely knit and well-developed system of time-space relationships of the pre-Columbian civilizations. Neither had ever heard of the other, nor had any suspicion that the other group existed. Western historiographers have studied the conquest from the justifying viewpoint of the European colonizers, but there is another perspective, that of the conquered. With the conquest, the world of the indigenous peoples of Mexico had, in effect, come to an end. The final battles in 1521 were not just a victory in warfare, but the end of a civilization. At first, some tribes welcomed the Spaniards and joined them in the hope of being liberated from Aztec domination. Only after the conquest did they discover that the defeat of the Aztecs was in effect the defeat of all the natives of their land. This painful calvary of the Mexican people began when Cortés landed on Good Friday, April 22, 1519. It ended with the final battle on August 13, 1521. It was a military as well as a theological overthrow, for their capital had been conquered, their women violated, their temples destroyed, and their gods defeated.

We cannot allow the cruelty of the conquest to keep us from appreciating the heroic efforts of the early missioners. Their writings indicated that it was their intention to found a new Christianity more in conformity with the Gospel, not simply a continuation of that in Europe. They had been carefully prepared by the universities of Spain. Immediate efforts were made to evangelize the native Mexicans. The lifestyle of the missioners, austere poverty and simplicity, was in stark contrast to that of the conquistadors. Attempts were made to become one with the people and to preach the Gospel in their own language and through their customs and traditions. Yet the missioners were limited by the socioreligious circumstances of their time. Dialogue was severely limited, since neither side understood the other. The Spaniards judged the Mexican world from within the categories of their own Spanish world vision. Iberian communication was based on philosophical and theological abstractions and direct, precise speech. The missioners were convinced that truth in itself was sufficient to bring rational persons to conversion. They were not aware of the totally different way of communicating truth, especially divine truth, which the native Mexicans believed could be adequately communicated only through flower and song. Even the best of the missioners could not penetrate the living temple of the Mexican consciousness.

This was also the time of the first *audiencia* of Guzmán, which was noted for its corruption and abuses of the Indians. During this period the church was in constant conflict with the civil authorities because of these authorities' excessive avarice, corruption, and cruel treatment of the natives. The friars were good men who gradually won the love and respect of the common people. However, the religious convictions of generations would not give way easily, especially those of a people who firmly believed that the traditions of their ancestors were the way of the gods. As the friars tried to convert the wise men of the Indians by well-prepared theological exposition, the Indians discovered that the friars were in effect trying to eliminate the religion of their ancestors. The shock of human sacrifices led many of the missioners to see everything else in the native religion as diabolical, whereas the shock of the Spaniards' disregard for life by killing in war kept the Indians from seeing anything good or authentic in the conquerors' religion. This mutual scandal made communication difficult. Furthermore, the painful memory of the conquest and new hardships imposed upon the Indians made listening to a "religion of love" difficult. Efforts to communicate remained at the level of words, but never seemed to penetrate to the level of the symbols of the people, which contained the inner meanings of their world vision. For the Indians these attempts at conversion by total rupture with the ways of their ancestors were a deeper form of violence than the physical conquest itself.

— "Our Lady of Guadalupe as a Cultural Symbol," 26–27

ERUPTION OF DIVINE COMPASSION

In his spiritual writings on the Guadalupe apparition account Virgilio seeks to empathize with the conquered native peoples and discern the significance of Guadalupe's love and message from their perspective. His conclusion is that to the indigenous Guadalupe must have appeared as nothing less than a compassionate and gratuitous intervention of God to alleviate their suffering, a source of hope and new life for a vanquished people who sought her maternal care and protection. The following passage explicates these convictions in the context of narrating Juan Diego's encounters with Guadalupe.

Place yourself for a moment in the position of the conquered people. They had been devastated. Everything that was of value to them had been destroyed. And now the missionaries of the God of the conquistadors, missionaries who were very holy and saintly men, came in and began to proclaim a Gospel of love, of compassion, and of forgiveness. The people could not understand them. They were the missionaries of the same group that just slaughtered the people and they practiced the same religion. When the priests spoke about love and compassion and understanding and generosity, the people could not comprehend. How could these men speak of a God so opposite from their experience? ...

In some ways the missionaries were the agents of the ultimate violence because they were agents of religious violence. There is nothing deeper for people than their religious roots — their God-imagery. When the chosen people were slaves in Egypt, the first thing they asked was to worship in their own way. Nothing is deeper for people than that.

Recently I was in Germany doing some workshops for the Spanish-speaking military, discussing Hispanic–United States relations within the military. We had a good discussion — all in English. Everyone spoke English perfectly. Toward the end of the meeting a woman raised her hand tentatively and I asked if she wanted to say something. She said, "Well, no, maybe not. Maybe not really." I said, "Go ahead, what did you want to say?" She said, "Well, I'm sort of embarrassed to say it but I really want to ask, since the time is almost over, would you lead us in saying a 'Hail Mary' in Spanish?" I said, "Certainly." So we all got up and said a "Dios te salve María" in Spanish. A number of people started to cry. Several came up afterward and said that it was the deepest religious experience they had ever had since being in the military.

Never underestimate the power of our core religious imagery, of our core religious symbolism. Theology is second level — at the head level. At the gut level, what imagery puts me in communion with my God? At this level the missionaries, without intending to be, were the agents of the ultimate violence, defending the people but doing violence among them by uprooting the images of their gods. ...

Into that setting comes an incredible eruption of God's goodness. It always happens that way. The God of the Bible, as
Raymond Brown has said so beautifully, is always the God
of unexpected surprises — the God who comes through in a
way that we could only begin to suspect or imagine. It was an
incredible surprise that the Son of God would become flesh as
a Galilean. Everyone knew that nothing good could come out
of Galilee. The God of the Bible is always the God who acts in
ways that you and I can only begin to imagine or suspect. And
once again, in the midst of this incredible hell of suffering created through our own efforts to conquer and become great at
the cost of others, the God of goodness, the God of the Bible,
the God who hears the cries of the poor, the God of the exodus,
the God who sees the suffering of the afflicted, and the God
who says, "I am going to save my people" — that God made
an eruption.

The worst battle of the conquest took place in 1521. During the following years the people wanted only to die. Now in
1531, only ten years later, in the context of a massive death
wish, this incredible eruption of God takes place in such a simple way that it is reminiscent of the birth narratives of the
Gospels of Jesus.

A simple Indian — not just an Indian but the lowest class
Indian — was walking to church where he was a catechu-
men, and he heard beautiful music. He heard such beautiful
singing that he thought he had died and was awakening in paradise. In the Aztec Indian world, life is a dream and death is
the awakening. So he thought that he had awakened and was
in the presence of the divine. He was listening to this beautiful singing and music and a Lady appeared. The words in
the original Indian narrative are fascinating. He saw a Lady
who was so beautiful she radiated like the sun and she spoke
to him in the most tender way. She called him "My dearest
Juan" — "Juanito," which means "one who is closest to me."
She introduced herself by saying, "I am the mother of the true
God through whom one lives." Then she told him to tell the

bishop that the mother of the true God through whom one lives wanted the bishop to build a temple here at Tepeyac hill. So Juan went excitedly to the bishop with the good news of this beautiful vision. But when he tried to see the bishop he got the runaround. Finally he saw the bishop and told him the story. The bishop listened to him but was indifferent. So he returned feeling very rejected because he had failed the Lady. Then comes one of the most beautiful parts of the narrative. Feeling inferior and unworthy he went back to the Lady and said, "You know, the bishop didn't listen to me. I am just a poor Indian. I am nothing. I am worse than a bunch of dried-up worms or broken sticks. I am nobody. Send somebody who is important, somebody who is well known and respectable." But the Lady told him, "My son, I have many messengers whom I could pick. I have many ambassadors whom I could choose. But it is in every way necessary that you, the smallest of my children, be my messenger to the bishop. I want you to go."

So he went back and this time the bishop listened a bit more and asked him for a sign. The bishop was surprised when the Indian did not hesitate. He said, "Of course I will bring you the sign." So he ran back and told the Lady, who said, "Come back tomorrow and I will give you the sign." So he went home, and when he arrived he found that his uncle was sick and dying. He decided that he would get a priest to come and anoint his uncle in the last rites before going to the Lady. Here it almost becomes a comedy. He went around the other side of the hill so the Lady would not stop him. He had to get a priest, and so he went around the other side of the hill. To his amazement the Lady stopped him. He was embarrassed and apologetic and said, "I really was not running out on you but I have to get a priest for my uncle." The Lady assured him that his uncle was well and that he was to go up and get the sign which was waiting for him. So he went up to the top of the barren hill and there he found the most beautiful roses. He cut the roses and put them in his *tilma* [cloak] and took them to the bishop. And the bishop finally saw them. When the flowers fell to the ground the image appeared on the *tilma* for the bishop and everyone to see.

— "Mary and Evangelization," 148–50, 152–54

THROUGH THE EYES OF JUAN DIEGO

Just as God became human as Jesus the Galilean who pronounced good news among the Galileans of his day, so too Our Lady of Guadalupe came to Juan Diego as one of his own people and rejuvenated the life of the conquered natives. The following selection is one of many in which Virgilio shows that the encounters between Guadalupe and Juan Diego illuminate Gospel dynamics like choosing the rejected and offering them new life and purpose. Italicized citations in this selection are translations from the Nican Mopohua *narrative of the Guadalupe apparitions.*

...all kinds of exquisite flowers from Castile, open and flowering.

With the very first appearance of the Virgin, everything begins to change; everything is transformed; everything takes on a new look. Like the first buds of a new spring, initiating a new cycle of life, her presence will produce a new, beautiful, and exquisite flowering upon earth.

In her presence, Juan Diego experiences a new sense of being while all the things on the barren desert hill take on a new appearance: the rocks appear like emeralds and other precious stones; the earth shines like the rainbow; the cacti and other brush looked like the beautiful feathers of the precious birds; and the leaves and even the thorns of the trees seem to be made of gold. In her presence, everything takes on a new light and fragrance. The innermost beauty and dignity of all creation become manifest in her presence. What is happening? What is she capable of bringing about?

*He saw a lady who was standing and who was calling him
to come closer to her side.... He marveled at her perfect
beauty.... Her clothing appeared like the sun, and it gave
forth rays.*

Who is La Virgen for Juan Diego and subsequently for the millions of people across the ages, the Americas, and the oceans
who have looked upon her merciful presence? The answers are
too many and varied to deal with them here. We can begin
to explore the matter, however, by examining how she first
appears and how she introduces herself.

... "Dignified Juan, dignified Juan Diego."

The very sound of the voice of a person reveals much about
that person and her or his mood in relation to us — anger,
arrogance, righteousness, authority, fear, indifference, concern,
doubt, confidence, friendship, peace, tranquility. Humans communicate not just through words but also through the way they
say those words. The very manner in which we speak to people
reveals our inner attitude toward them and allows them to
experience proximity or distance, concern or burden, familiarity
or contempt, confidence or distrust, and many other attitudes.
The very tone of voice communicates the position of the heart
while the way in which we address them indicates what we
think of them: friend, parent, superior, servant, and so on.

The first revelation of La Virgen's identity comes through the
very way she addresses Juan Diego. She is one who provokes
intimacy and affection. There is no indication in the narrative
that Juan Diego was in any way fearful when he first heard
her call. The natural anxiety that such an exceptional experience would produce is immediately calmed by the reassuring
tenderness of her voice. Her voice is affirming, compassionate,
and inviting. In her presence, there is no fear. Quite the con-
trary, there is immediate acceptance and familiarity. Juan Diego
is addressed not as *Indio* or with the generic *tu* (you) but by
name. Rather than being put down, he is dignified by the very

way in which he is addressed. There is no command issued, only an invitation offered. Furthermore, his name is uttered with the greatest respect, familiarity, and affection. He is being treated not as a child (as the missioners treated the Indians) but as a full and mature human being. This mirrors the manner of the presence of Jesus among the poor and marginalized masses of his time.

He . . . heard her thought and word, which were exceedingly re-creative, very ennobling, alluring, producing love.

By her very voice, she lets us know that in her presence, we have nothing to fear; we have nothing to be ashamed of; we have nothing to worry about — for she knows us well, and she calls us by name to come to her side that she might be our faithful and loving companion. Her identity is brought out in her very first greeting and then throughout her ongoing conversations with Juan Diego. She will be our constant companion throughout the tribulations of life, giving life to our struggles and comfort in our tribulations.

But this Lady who is calling Juan by name in a very respectful and loving way is not just any ordinary person — Spaniard or Indian. Everything about her reveals her very special nature and identity.

He marveled at her perfect beauty. Her clothing appeared like the sun, and it gave forth rays.

Juan Diego is fascinated by what he sees. She is of perfect beauty, and her clothes radiate like the sun — in fact, it seems the very sun radiates out of her. No wonder he thinks he might be in heaven, the source of life and light. She is both radically unlike the Indian divinities (e.g., she is not distant and unapproachable, as the human-god Montezuma had been) and yet similar to them in some ways. The sun was the Nahuatl symbol of God, the God through whom one lives and is maintained in existence. But she is even greater than their God, for she covers the sun, while not extinguishing it; she stands upon the moon (the other manifestation of the deity) but does not crush it; so she will tell the Indians (and us) something beautiful and unsuspected about God (like Paul at the Areopagus [Acts 17:16–34], who tells the Greeks about their unknown God); she will tell them and the church more about God than they had known or suspected. She does not destroy the natives' gods nor deny the God of Christians but presents something much more attractive and humanizing — both to the Indians and to the Christians of that moment of history and even today. She does not look like any of the natives' gods: she is so human, yet she radiates divinity. This was a great and startling mystery — totally human and yet so evidently divine.

The missioners wanted to destroy the Indians' sacred statues and replace them with Euro-Christian imagery. She offers something totally new and inclusive of the statues of the natives and images of the Christians. She is no mere Indian statue or Christian image, for she has a pleasant voice that speaks the very language of the people. Even more, she has a compassionate face and beautiful eyes in which Juan Diego could see himself reflected in a loving, respected, and accepted way. She speaks their language and looks upon them with love, understanding, and compassion. The beauty and perfection of her eyes continue to fascinate scholars to this day.

Her very presence brings about the experience of God. She is of the divine order but is also simple and unassuming. She does not provoke terror or anxiety, only comfort and joy. Because of her appearance, there is no doubt that she is of the highest nobility, but she does not sit on a throne or stool as, respectively, the Spanish or Indian nobility often did when presiding over their subjects. There are no pretenses of superiority, she simply wants to be among her people. She simply stands before Juan Diego as an equal, invites him to her side, and initiates the conversation in a very friendly and egalitarian way.

When Juan Diego sees her for the first time, she is divinely beautiful and definitely one of his own brown-skinned, brown-eyed, and black-haired people. She is of the highest nobility, but she comes out of the very earth of the native peoples. In her, heaven and earth are once again in harmony. The floral imagery on her dress is typical of Indian decoration and symbolic of the interconnectedness of all creation. Her face, her features, and her dress are proper to an Indian woman at that time who was with child. The glyph of the Aztec calendar right over her womb indicates that she is the mother of the baby Sun, the mother of the new life about to be inaugurated upon these lands. Her own words will bring this out when she tells Juan Diego that she will be the mother of all the inhabitants of these lands.

We speak about Guadalupe as an apparition, but it is really much more of an *encuentro,* a coming together of two friends. It is analogous to the encounter-appearances of the Risen Lord with his apostles. This is a person-to-person conversation, something quite different from the dealings the Indians had with the friars, which were definitely between the inferior student and the superior teacher. Juan has not worked for this gift. It is a gratuitous gift from God, and Juan responds enthusiastically.

— *Guadalupe: Mother of the New Creation,* 60–65

A GIFT OF LOVE

Gratitude is fundamental to the spiritual life. It is the profound sense that I have been given something for no other reason than because I am loved. In the following passage Virgilio evokes this sense of wondrous gratitude for God's gift of Our Lady of Guadalupe.

What is her power? What is her compelling force? What is the logic of Guadalupe devotion which seems to defy our systems of logic and reasoning? What is the inner force that continues to make her so alive and important for us?

Ask yourself: What is the power of a precious gift given to us by someone we love?

I suspect, in a simple way, its innermost power is that it is a gift from God. Protestants tell me: "But Christ alone is necessary for salvation." And I say to them: "You are absolutely right. That is precisely what makes Guadalupe so precious. Precisely because she is not necessary, she is so special! She is a gift of God's love."

Aren't the most precious things in our lives the gifts that were given to us? They are so precious precisely because they were not necessary. How often have we told someone we love: "You don't have to give me anything!" Yet the lover insists, and we treasure the gift. Life would be so dull if it were reduced to only the absolutely necessary things in life and salvation itself would become mechanical reduced to only that which is necessary.

I suspect that is one reason why I love our popular Catholic tradition of processions, devotions, relics, candles, holy water, and other sacramentals. It is the whole complex of these many "unnecessary" manifestations of God's love that allows God's love to appear so plentiful, personal, and beautiful.

Recall the help of a teacher or coach, or the little extras your parents or grandparents gave you, or a friend or even a stranger who was there for you in a moment of need. Look at the many "unnecessary" things which became so important in your life. Just think what incredible power you have to bring about that richness of life within others.

The expanding power and force of Guadalupe is that it is a precious gift of God's love to the people of the Americas at the very moment it started to become the land of the great encounter of all the peoples of the world.

— *A Retreat with Our Lady of Guadalupe
and Juan Diego, 81–82*

IMAGO DEI

Virgilio relates in the following meditation that, for the indigenous peoples, the beauty enveloping Guadalupe reflected both the feminine face of God and the divinely cherished face of human persons. In the Americas, Guadalupe initiates a profoundly incarnated expression of the Gospel proclamation about God, humanity, and the saving message of Jesus Christ.

What is the meaning of Guadalupe? When Juan Diego was walking to church, he heard beautiful music. He heard such beautiful singing that he thought he had died and gone to heaven. At the end of the story he presented the sign to the bishop, and the sign was flowers — flowers more beautiful than anyone had ever seen. In the Indian understanding this divine revelation took place in the context of music and flowers. For the Indian world, the main category for the divine was the beautiful. You did not speak about God in rational terms. You spoke about God in terms of beauty, in terms that were only suggestive because God is God. God is beyond all of my categories. And so we cannot corral God into a dictionary definition or the definition of a theological dogma. God is God and therefore God is greater than my expressions of God. Only in the power of music and flowers can we communicate the divine. The Guadalupe story begins with the sign of music and ends with the sign of flowers. Therefore, for the Indian world, they are no longer just human. Divinity is erupting and speaking to them in a way they can understand.

Secondly, the Lady appears at Tepeyac. Tepeyac had been the most sacred site of the Indian mother goddess, the earth goddess. It had been the site of pilgrimages from faraway lands from time immemorial. Different tribes came to venerate the sanctuary of the earth goddess, who had her sanctuary at Tepeyac. It was the custom of the Spaniards to rename every sacred site of the Indians, and they had renamed this site Guadalupe because there is a shrine of Guadalupe in Spain. Our Lady of Guadalupe in Spain had been the patroness of the reconquest of Spain against the Arabs, and then she had been the patroness of Cortés who came to the Americas. It was at Tepeyac, the famous shrine of the mother goddess, that the

Lady appeared and told him, "I am the mother of the true God, through whom one lives."

The true God was the Spanish understanding of God but the term was incomprehensible to the Indian world. For them the imagery of God was the one through whom one lives. For the Indian world, nothing would exist if God took power away from it. We exist only because God sustains our existence. Therefore their term for God was "the one through whom one lives." The Spanish concept of God was incomprehensible to the Indians and the Indian concept of God was abominable to the Spaniards. The Lady united the Spanish concept with the Indian concept in one image of God. She began to unite what appeared to be two irreconcilable religions. She began a profound incarnation of the Gospel.

The mother of the true God through whom one lives radiates divinity. She radiates the sun and begins to usher in the maternal, the female, aspect of the deity. For the Indian world a god that was exclusively male was incomprehensible. A god that was exclusively male could not be a god because it would be incomplete. The God that the European Christians presented was strongly and exclusively a male God. For the Indian world there was always the Father God who acted and the Mother God who asked. And the two always acted in concert. The Mother asked and the Father gave, but the Father would not give what the Mother would not ask for. In the message of Guadalupe you have the Mother who listens to her children to remedy all their miseries, their pain, and suffering. The Mother is listening so that she might present, and when the Mother presents the Father cannot deny. It is a powerful duality that is understood by the simple people. When you ask many of our people, "Why is devotion to Mary so important to you?" they will respond, "Oh, Father, the church is so complicated. The Mother is so simple."

I have been pastor of a downtown parish for five years. It is a great sanctuary of poor people coming to pray. I have learned more about the imagery of God and about prayer from them than I had ever learned before. It is true when Jesus, in the Gospels of Matthew and Luke, praises the Father because what is hidden from the wise and the intelligent has been revealed to the little ones (Matt. 11:25, Luke 10:21). This is the mother in the Gospel of John who, with her mother's intuition, notices that they are running out of wine and presents it to Jesus because she knows Jesus will act (John 2:1–11). This is the true mother of the God through whom one lives and her greatest gift is her son. In the Guadalupe image Mary is not carrying a child. You do not see the child in the Guadalupe image but it is there. If you look at it very carefully, right over the womb of Guadalupe you will see the Aztec Indian symbol for the center of the universe. Guadalupe presents herself with a black band around her waist, which is a sign of maternity — a sign that she is carrying a child. You will also see that her cheeks are the cheeks of a woman in about the third month of pregnancy. They retain a lot of water. Guadalupe appears with a Christ child in her womb because the greatest gift she will give will be the new center of the universe, the new center of our life, which is Christ the Lord. So she is a perfectly Christocentric presentation of a new beginning who will listen to the people and be among them to help and to guide them.

But this Lady who is the mother of the true God through whom one lives, this Lady who appears as the divine revelation, is herself not a goddess. For the Indian world the gods were always beyond our power to know. Therefore they always wore a mask and had no eyes to see. In Guadalupe a beautiful face appears that not only can be seen but has eyes that see you and me. When you study the eye of Guadalupe under a microscope you see the figure of a person in that eye. That figure is not Juan Diego as many feel that it is. In 1531 it was Juan Diego but at this moment the power of Guadalupe is that everyone who looks on her in faith sees himself or herself reflected in an accepting way in her eye. The image of the human person in Guadalupe's eye is the image of you and of me. Generations of people have seen themselves accepted by the mother of the true

God through whom one lives. That is the power of Guadalupe to lift up the downtrodden, to give them a new dignity, a new self-appreciation, and to move them forward. It is this Lady who picks the Indian, the one whom the world says has nothing to offer, the one whom the world says is a minor. And she tells the Indian, "You are to be my most trusted messenger...."

Guadalupe begins the true incarnation of the liberating and empowering message of Jesus in the Americas. As Hellenistic Christianity once opened the doors for the Gospel to go into new areas of the world that it had not yet touched, Guadalupe Christianity today opens the possibility for new understandings of God — for understanding the femininity of God and for understanding the treasure the peoples contribute to make Christianity more faithful to the Gospel and to the people. The theological and ecclesial structures of the West have difficulty understanding this. This new church of the people is not in opposition to, but is a source of enrichment for, the total universal church. As we begin to go into the third millennium we will find, in the ranks of the poor and the suffering who have no strength and dignity except in their God and the mother of their God, new expressions of the Gospel that will enrich all of us.

Today devotion to Our Lady of Guadalupe continues to grow, to be explored, and to be rediscovered. Our explanations do not make it powerful. It is powerful because it lives in the minds and hearts of the people. It is a fire that is pulling the people together in spite of all obstacles, and is offering them new imagery into universal Christianity that I believe will enrich and unite all the peoples of the third millennium.

— "Mary and Evangelization," 155–57, 160

LIVING TRADITION

The Guadalupe encounter is not merely an ancient tradition but an ongoing bond with millions of her faithful daughters

*and sons. Annually her December 12 feast renews and expands
this bond. Numerous devotees who have known the pain of
rejection such as* mestizos *and immigrants resonate with the
dramatic proclamation of the lowly Juan Diego's rejection, his
encounter with a loving mother, and his final vindication. She
continues to appear in the daily lives of her people and accompanies them in their struggles for dignity, justice, and life. For
countless devotees the core experience of Guadalupe is the repli-
cation of Juan Diego's intimate, mystical encounter with their
celestial mother. In their conversations, prayers, and sustained
gazes at her image, devotees relive this mystical encounter. Our
Lady of Guadalupe incites the communion of* mestizaje, *uniting
diverse peoples as sisters and brothers in the veneration of their
loving mother. The following passage explores the expanding
dynamism of the Guadalupe tradition.*

Every year on December 12, very early in the morning before
the first rays of the sun break the darkness of the night, in
continuity with our native ancestors who gathered each day
to welcome the rising of the new sun and with early Christians who gathered early on Easter Sunday to welcome the first
day of the new creation, Mexicans and Mexican Americans
gather in great numbers to dance the rituals of the ancient *matachines* [native dances] and sing the *mañanitas* [morning songs]
to the brown virgin of Guadalupe. We gather to welcome the
new creation, the birth of our race, the *mestizo* people of the
Americas.

   Devotion to Our Lady of Guadalupe, the queen, empress,
and mother of the Americas, expresses the deepest nationality of our people. I remember vividly and still look forward
to celebrating today the great festivities surrounding the feast
of Guadalupe: from the preparatory novenas, to the all-night
dances of the *matachines,* to the predawn massive gathering for
the singing of the *mañanitas,* to the evening offering of flowers
and crowning of our queen. She is not the museum-like queen of

Fiesta San Antonio,* but the living queen-mother of life whose love and compassion continue to reign within our hearts. As I work on this manuscript, children from throughout my parish are outside learning the ritual dances from their parents. Each generation passes on to the next the thread of life that binds us to our ancestors and projects us into the future. The annual celebration of the Guadalupe event is not just a devotion or a large church gathering. It is the collective affirmation and cultic celebration of life in spite of the multiple threats of death.

In Catholic elementary school they would tell us about the *real* apparitions — Lourdes, Fatima. The apparition of the Americas at Tepeyac was casually referred to as Mexican folklore, an affair of the Indians, the religiosity of the uninformed. But in my home parish, Christ the King, the Virgin of Guadalupe was celebrated in ways no other religious feast in the Catholic calendar was celebrated. In those days I did not know about the hierarchy of feasts in the official calendar of the church, but in my own experience, there was no question that the main feast of the year was that of Our Lady of Guadalupe.

Her presence was not only celebrated in the churches, but she reigned maternally in all our homes, our places of business, our cars and buses, and even over the heads of the pilots in modern-day jets. Her medal is worn over the hearts of millions of her children, and many young soldiers going to war had her image tattooed on their bodies to insure their protection. Her banner has led and given courage to all the major efforts for liberation of the Mexican people — from the flag of the war of [Mexican] independence of Father [Miguel] Hidalgo in 1810 to the present-day struggles of César Chávez with the farm workers in California.

---

*Fiesta San Antonio is a weeklong series of festivities celebrated throughout San Antonio every April. Its origins are the Battle of Flowers Parade that prominent Anglo-American women first organized in 1891 to commemorate the April 21, 1836, Texas victory over Mexican forces, which established Texas independence from Mexico.

She not only appeared on the outskirts of Mexico City in December of 1531, but she continues to appear today throughout the Americas in the art, the poetry, the dramas, the anthropological studies, the religious expressions, the shrines, and the pilgrimages of her people. Rather than saying that she appeared in 1531, it would be more accurate to say that she started to appear — to be present among us — in 1531 and that her visible, tangible, and motherly presence continues to spread throughout the Americas.

Her story is not only retold with the same reverence as the Gospel stories, but dramatic presentations continue to reflect upon the liberating power that she is capable of transmitting to her children. It continues to fascinate believers and unbelievers alike. It continues to draw together peoples of all backgrounds — rich and poor, Mexican and U.S., white and brown, Protestant and Catholic. She is a sacred icon whose power is far beyond our abilities of comprehension but whose life-giving power and liberating influence are at the very core of our untiring struggles for survival and new life.…

But beyond all my explanation and the pious or cynical interpretations of others, the power and force of the devotion continues to increase throughout the Americas. In any major city in the United States December 12 is celebrated each year with the greatest joy and solemnity. It is commemorated with processions, dances, songs, presentations of the original experience, Masses, crownings. The impact of her presence attracts the masses of the faithful, but it equally attracts the attention of theologians, historians, and scientists. It is not an event that happened only some 475 years ago, but an event that continues to transform millions of people throughout the Americas today. The full meaning of Guadalupe cannot be adequately explained, but it can be experienced.

Guadalupe has a magnetic power to attract diverse people from all walks of life and, in her, they can experience unity. The basis of this unity is not the feeling that one often has at large gatherings, that of being absorbed by the mob. The deepest basis of the humanizing unity is that regardless of the magnitude of the crowds, in her presence each individual experiences personal recognition. Each one is looked upon compassionately, eye-to-eye, and tenderly called by name.

— *The Future Is Mestizo*, 57–59, 65–66

FORETASTES OF HEAVEN

All of us who are baptized as disciples of Jesus have been called to the evangelizing mission of proclaiming Christ in word and deed. The following selection presents a vision of evangelization rooted in "foretastes of heaven" as revealed in Juan Diego's encounter with Our Lady of Guadalupe, in the celebration of the Eucharist, and in the fervor and joy of the poor whose trust in God overshadows their daily struggles.

The apparition of Our Lady of Guadalupe is the beginning of the new evangelization, the one that Paul VI spoke about in 1975 [in the apostolic exhortation *Evangelii Nuntiandi*] and John Paul II has been so urgently calling for as the millennium comes to an end. We might summarize the evangelizing method, expression, and fervor of the Guadalupe process by stating that it proceeded by way of beauty, initiated a gradual dialogue, was most respectful of the evangelized, and empowered them with new life. Because it invited the evangelized to an experience of the divine, into a mystical experience, it produced security, joy, and excitement. It did not just speak about God and the teachings of God; it invited the participant into intimate contact and friendship with God. This mystical experience of the presence of God is at the core of the new evangelization.

The method of Guadalupe is based on beauty, recognition and respect for "the other," and friendly dialogue. It is based on the power of attraction, not on threats of any kind. Juan Diego is attracted by the beautiful singing that he hears; he is fascinated by the gentleness and friendliness of the Lady, who by her appearance is evidently an important person; he is uplifted by her respectful and tender treatment of him; he is captivated by her looks. She is so important, yet she takes time to call him by name and to visit with him in a very friendly way. In her presence, he exhibits no inferiority or fears. Here there is no fear of hell; here, Juan Diego is experiencing heaven.

The old evangelization emphasized threats of hell and eternal damnation. Our Lady prefers to offer us a foretaste of heaven. This is the new method, which is actually the method of Jesus and which is supposed to be lived out in the Eucharist. The contrast between the old and the new is sharp. While the church was trying desperately to create vivid imagery of judgment, purgatory, and the eternal fires of hell, Our Lady of Guadalupe is giving Juan Diego a holistic experience of heaven. In her presence, he is transformed. And the final proof of the absolute truth of this experience is not the power and might of God proven in battle by the sword and the gun, but beautiful flowers with a heavenly aroma blooming on the desert hilltop — and in the midst of winter! The ultimate sign of God's transforming power is the peaceful and miraculous flowing of new life in the midst of the deserts of human existence, not the destructive power of the growing military might of the modern world. The powerful had crucified Jesus, had executed him unjustly, but God raised him to life. The sign of this power of God has always been the beautiful flowers of Easter. Flowers, not weapons, are the signs of God's ultimate power over unjust executions and death.

Juan Diego was re-created through his contacts with the Lady. This was the basis of his enthusiasm, courage, and fervor. He goes hurriedly, with confidence and joy, to the bishop's house. When today's poor experience themselves as recognized, respected, and called by name by the living God, they take on God's cause for humanity with the same joy and conviction as Juan Diego. They are no longer victims and are now survivors. Their fiestas, dances, songs, poetry, and joy make God's presence come alive. This type of evangelizing ministry is working miracles in ordinary pastoral life in parishes throughout the Americas. I have experienced this joy and fervor among the early *cursillistas,* the charismatics, the people who participate in the *comunidades de base,* the people who participated in civil rights demonstrations, and the many new movements of the Spirit that are erupting spontaneously throughout the Christian world. This joy and fervor erupt when the faithful poor dare to defy the controlling and limiting rules and regulations of the dominant culture and its religious institutions and dare to converse directly with God in their own language and in the language of their ancestors. It is the joy of the poor who, far from giving in to despair, rejoice in recognizing the unique gifts God has bestowed upon them. A true Christian fiesta cannot be programmed or faked. It is experienced and lived.

In evangelization, the church should be less concerned with the fires of hell, which are all too evident all around us, and with rules and regulations, which are so overwhelming in our bureaucratic society. It should be concerned, rather, with creating foretastes of heaven here on earth.

— *Guadalupe: Mother of the New Creation,* 119–20

CONVERTED BY BEAUTY

The following sermon for the Guadalupe feast uncovers the dynamics of conversion in the Gospels and in the Guadalupe apparitions narrative. It reveals that the pathway of conversion is not the same for all, though the call to conversion and transformation is extended to every disciple. It also ends this chapter fittingly, with Virgilio's prayer for our transformation so that we might build the living temple of a harmonious humanity that Our Lady of Guadalupe and her son Jesus Christ ask of us.

Just as the child in Elizabeth's womb leaped for joy upon hearing the greeting of Mary, so did Juan Diego and subsequently millions of persons throughout the ages who have encountered

Nuestra Señora del Tepeyac. So it is truly proper that on her feast day we gather to praise and thank God for this marvelous gift to all the inhabitants of this land we call America. It is so precious because at a moment of devastating human pain, our loving God sent us this precious gift to soothe our pain and begin the healing. But the Guadalupe event would do much more than just heal: it would actually be the beginning — the birth — of something so beautiful that it had never before happened in the course of human history. It would be much more than the beginning of a new world; it would truly mark the beginning of a new humanity. The gift of Our Lady of Guadalupe to America is especially precious because God did not have to do this, yet God, out of the abundance of God's compassionate love and fascinating creativity, wanted to do this for us, for humanity. Through her, the pains and scandal of conquest would be transformed into the joy and glory of new life.

Yet it was not just a gift for the people of that time. It is a gift to all of us at every moment of our collective earthly pilgrimage, while equally a very personal gift to each one of us. A loving mother loves all her children, but the "all" does not replace the very special love and concern she has for each one in particular.

I am sure that if you were to ask any mother for her greatest wish it would be that all her children could gather together and get along well with one another. She would not want to make them all the same, but she would rejoice in the uniqueness of each one and their capacity to get along well with each other and help each other in any way possible. This was precisely the wish of our Blessed Mother when she appeared at Tepeyac in 1531. She wanted a temple — a home — where she could gather together all her children, all the inhabitants of this land. She did not ask for a home just for the native peoples, nor just for the Europeans or the Africans who were already arriving, nor even for the mixed-race *mestizo* children who were beginning to be born. She wanted a home — a temple — for all her children, all the inhabitants of these lands. A more radical and refreshing word could not have been proclaimed by anyone. No one would have dared or even wanted to make such a proclamation, for racial and ethnic divisions were the accepted and enforced order of the day. No one but the mother of infinite love made flesh could have dared to make such a proclamation.

The reality at this moment of history was that in these lands recently discovered by Europeans, people were being divided into all kinds of social classes: masters, craftsmen, servants, slaves, women, men, whites, brown natives, *mestizos, mulatos,* blacks, and many others. All kinds of classifications were being used to legitimize the segregation, subjugation, and exploitation of human beings. This went totally against the wishes of Our Lady, who did not want to see her children trampled upon, humiliated, and abused. In her eyes and heart, every single one of the inhabitants was equally human, beautiful, and dignified.

Would the solution be to turn the natives against the Europeans? Would it be to return to a pre-European past? There was no return, of course, but whatever the injustices and pain of their indigenous past, the present appeared far worse. To the native peoples, it appeared to be hell on earth. In fact, hell could not have been worse. So, what was to be done?

In past times, the great gift of God's compassionate love in Jesus started when Mary of Nazareth said an unqualified "yes" to God's incomprehensible request that she become the mother of Jesus without having known man. She was asked to do the impossible. Through Mary's "yes" the almighty and omnipotent God took on flesh and was born as every other human being has been born! It was through Mary's "yes" that infinite love became human flesh with all the limitations, frailties, fears, and even temptations that are part of our human condition. And it was through this infinite love made flesh that God started the most marvelous adventure for the salvation of humanity.

Through the acceptance of Mary of Nazareth to be the mother of the redeemer, God had started the rehabilitation of our world, broken and dehumanized by centuries of sin. So too once again, at the beginning of this "new world" that had begun through the sinful greed and cruelty of men who would rob their victims of their fundamental dignity and worth, God sent God's own mother, Mary of Guadalupe, to begin the reconstruction of this horrible and chaotic mess. Sinful desires were behind the attempt of some to build empires of pomp, excess, and wealth through the exploitation of the poor and enslaved, but love wanted to build a family of goodness and compassion....

Since the very beginning of the preaching of Jesus, the personal entrance into the reign of God, into the family of God's children, came about through the repentance and conversion that accompanied belief in the Good News. This entails a complete transformation in our ways of thinking and feeling, a transformation of both the mind and the heart. In the midst of the chaos brought about by sin, what does this repentance and conversion mean in 1531 and even today? What is the "Good News" that people are to believe in then and now?

The personal encounter with the celestial Lady on the summit of Mount Tepeyac and subsequently in the palace of the bishop brought about an incredible transformation within the minds and hearts of everyone. It dissolved the deepest and most impenetrable walls that kept people from entering as brothers and sisters into the household of God. Today, encounters with her continue to produce those same grace-filled effects.

For Juan Diego, his fellow conquered peoples, and any of us who feels inferior, unworthy, or undignified, Our Lady calls us to repent from the negative and dehumanizing images of ourselves. She calls us to believe in ourselves and accept that we too are created in God's own image. We must throw away the old self and put on the new one. Our Lady brings this about in a very human way: she engaged Juan Diego in intimate conversation and confided an important mission to him. She, the celestial mother of God, treated him like an equal. She treated him like a human being. In her presence, he is fully a human being. In her presence all the derogatory categories he has been subjected to dissolve and he experiences himself for what he truly is: a dignified and noble human being. This indeed is Good News!

We are not what the sinful world says that we are. Through the encounter with Our Lady, we recognize ourselves for what we truly are: beloved children of God.

For the native world, culture and tradition were passed on to the next generation by the maternal uncle. The dying Juan Bernardino symbolized the absolute end of the native traditions and culture. It seemed that their cherished ways of life would be gone forever. But as so often happens, God had other plans. In the healing of Juan Bernardino we see the restoration of the traditions and culture of the ancestors. They were not false or diabolical, nor were they opposed to the Christian faith. Their ways would indeed be converted to Christianity, many of their ways would be modified and even enriched, but not at the cost of abandoning the sacred ways of their ancestors. They would come into the Christian family not deposed of their cultural treasures, but rather enriched with the incarnation of Christianity in these lands. They in turn would enrich the universal Christian family with all the treasures of their spiritual heritage. Today, this is the uniqueness, beauty, and wealth of our *mestizo* Christianity — a rich blend of the medieval Christianity of Europe with the deeply religious traditions of native America.

This healing of Juan Bernardino — custodian and transmitter of tradition — is important for us today. Often, in the face of the dominant culture and the latest fashions and styles, we might begin to think that the traditions and customs of our parents and grandparents are backward, antiquated, and embarrassing. Yet our traditions are sacred. They are not perfect and beyond improvement, for no culture is without its expressions of sin. But they are sacred, beautiful, and life-giving, for they connect us with our roots, with the very roots of our earthly existence. So just as Our Lady healed Juan Bernardino and thus guaranteed the continuation of the native customs and traditions, she reinforces and brings new energy into our customs and traditions, which are constantly challenged and threatened by globalization and the dominant material cultures of today. Fidelity to Our Lady guarantees the survival of the ways of our ancestors creatively integrated with the advances of the modern world. This is certainly Good News, for we will neither disappear as a people nor be isolated from the rest of humanity. Rather, in the give and take with other peoples, we will continuously contribute to the growth and development of the new humanity — the temple of Our Lady wherein no one will ever be excluded. This indeed is joyful Good News.

Conversion to the Good News of Jesus is never final and absolute until we see our God face to face at the end of our earthly life. So the bishop, the one designated as the primary evangelizer of the new world, also had to be converted. If Juan Diego had to convert from not believing in himself to seeing himself as a full and dignified human being, Bishop Juan de Zumárraga, the Europeans who considered themselves superior to the natives, and all people who consider themselves superior to others are called to repent from the sin of arrogance. They are called to no longer think of themselves as more important, nobler, more dignified, more worthy, and therefore authorized to insult, ridicule, and subjugate others. Repent and convert! Here the "Good News" might at first appear as "bad news," for it will mean thinking less of ourselves. Yet it is in this letting go, in our willingness to think of ourselves as less than society makes us think of ourselves, that we will gain a new freedom to be truly ourselves. It will be difficult, yet most liberating and life-giving, for only in letting go of the categories of superior and inferior, dignified and undignified, worthy and unworthy, noble and commoner can we all confront the Juan de Zumárraga tendencies that lurk inside of us and enter into the joyful freedom of the children of God.

Our Lady, not through threats or condemnations, but through inspiring music, intimate conversations, and a beautiful self-portrait brings about the repentance, conversion, and belief that allows everyone to let go of their limiting and destructive self-images and see and appreciate themselves as God sees and appreciates all. The abiding presence of Our Lady invites each and every one of us into her family. She urges us to celebrate her feast in her home where we gather without any dehumanizing distinctions to celebrate the Eucharist in which her beloved son, Jesus Christ, continues to offer himself to us as the bread of eternal life and the one true source for the unity of humanity. She came to prepare the home where we could come and meet her son, who was and is the firstborn of the new creation: a humanity of radical equality and harmonizing unity. The repentance, conversion, and joyful belief we experience in the encounter with Nuestra Madrecita de Guadalupe del Tepeyac prepare us to receive her son into our lives in the table fellowship of her home.

In encountering Our Lady of Guadalupe today, we, like Juan Diego before us and all the peoples of previous generations, experience the joyful conversion to new life, to the life of the new humanity. Like Juan Diego, today we are invited to experience the beauty and delicacy of Our Lady's inviting presence so that we too will leap for joy, a joy that only God and God's mother are capable of producing in us.

Santa María de Guadalupe, come to us as you came to Juan Diego so that we might believe in ourselves as you believe in us. Come to us as you came to Juan Bernardino so that we might value, celebrate, and transmit the sacred traditions of our parents and grandparents. Come to us as you came to Bishop Juan de Zumárraga so that we might listen to the poor and simple of society and hear the call of God through their cries for recognition, understanding, and appreciation. Let us all work together to build that temple you requested: a space of universal welcome and fellowship for all the peoples of this hemisphere. Whether it is in our homes, our neighborhoods, our cities, our nations, or the world, let us do all we can to break down the walls of prejudice and build up the temple of the new humanity, a living temple of love and compassion. Let our untiring efforts become the beautiful and alluring melodies that will attract all peoples to your holy mountain and through you to the great banquet table of our Lord Jesus Christ.

— "Converted by Beauty," 73–78

4

Following Christ

The church...must implant itself among all these groups in the same way that Christ by his incarnation committed himself to the particular social and cultural circumstances of the women and men among whom he lived.

— *Ad Gentes*, no. 10

Ultimately, there is only one Christian spirituality: following Jesus Christ in his life, death, and resurrection. Specific Christian spiritualities such as those of the Franciscans, Benedictines, Carmelites, and lay ecclesial movements emphasize aspects of this one spirituality. They delve more deeply into particular elements of the way of Christ, though none of them can ever exhaust the mystery of his person or the mystery of our life with God.

Christian spirituality is a way of following Christ. It springs from the movement of the Holy Spirit in the life and prayer of disciples who strive to incarnate Jesus in a particular time and place. Spiritual writings stir the hearts of believers. They unveil and nurture the Spirit's inspiration. They illuminate a way — not "the way" but "a way" — that disciples seek to faithfully live the Gospel here and now.

Virgilio's writings discern and foster a pathway of discipleship in the life witness and experiences of his Mexican American mestizo people. He articulates Gospel commitments that can guide Mexican American leaders to follow Christ, from Galilee to Jerusalem to the new life of the resurrection. He examines the prayer traditions that formed them in faith. He acclaims the evangelical spirit that animates their dedication to loving Christ and their neighbor. He reflects on virtues and practices that are at the heart of their Christian living. Like other spiritual writers, he illuminates and nurtures a work of God's Spirit among Christian believers in the concrete circumstances of their history and daily reality. Yet, though deeply rooted in his own experience and that of his fellow Mexican Americans, his writings offer insight and wisdom to all who seek to follow Christ. This final chapter examines Virgilio's reflections on discipleship in our contemporary world.

ON THE STREETS
OF A FRAGILE WORLD

The following excerpt is a straightforward example of trying to imitate Christ in word and deed. It reveals Virgilio's strong devotion to encountering Christ in the Blessed Sacrament and asking the Lord to guide his life and ministry. It also illuminates that discipleship entails imitating the Gospel dynamics of Jesus' Galilean origins and ministry: recognizing the fundamental dignity of myself and others as God's children and becoming an instrument of Jesus' compassion for the rejected.

After many years I returned to the downtown as rector of San Fernando Cathedral. As I walked the same streets I had known growing up, I started to become aware of many things that I had never noticed before. Besides the downtown being somewhat run-down, the many closed stores and especially the closed movie houses I had enjoyed so much, there was something else that was very different. Maybe it had always been there, but I had never noticed it before.

Certainly there were many more tourists than locals walking around. This was indeed something new. But there was something else. I started to notice the presence of many homeless people, some drug peddlers, and many male and female prostitutes. I suspect they had been around all the time, but I had never been aware of them before. These people made the downtown their home and therefore they were my parishioners. I was supposed to be their pastor, but I had no preparation for dealing with them. So what should I do? How should I deal with them? Should I just avoid them? Should I chastise them and condemn them for their immorality? Should I go to the City Council and demand that they pass laws to "clean up the city"? I really did not know what to do.

So, in desperation, I went to my favorite counselor. After I had closed down the cathedral for the night and had it all to myself, I went to pray before the Blessed Sacrament. I have always experienced a great source of energy and wisdom emanating from the tabernacle. Call it magic if you wish, call it superstition or whatever. To me, since I was a little child, it has been the real presence of Jesus waiting to enter into deep conversation with me. I love to just kneel or sit there in silence and let my mind wander wherever it goes. I don't try to control or guide it, I just let myself be in the presence of the Master. Sometimes I even fall into a peaceful sleep. There is an incredible peace and serenity and illumination that gradually takes over — sometimes. Other times, it's just a terrific place to truly rest and relax.

There in the silence of the night, the cathedral glittering with hundreds of vigil lights burning and the city lights illuminating the stained-glass windows, answers to my pastoral dilemma began to become clear to me. How did Jesus deal with persons similar to the ones I was encountering? How did he deal with the Samaritan woman? With the centurion who wanted his boy to be healed? With the public sinners and prostitutes he encountered?

Jesus did not chastise the people in the margins who were looked upon as the public sinners of society; he entered into conversation with them, treated them as persons, befriended them, and invited them into his company. By so doing, he enabled them to recognize what society had denied them: their fundamental human dignity and infinite worth! This was the beginning of their change, this was the "good news": they were not worthless whores or bums, but human beings. Jesus was not afraid to shock and scandalize all the good and pious people of his time who found it so easy to judge, classify, and condemn but so impossible to accept, understand, and appreciate.

Who is not broken in some way or another? Wounded people need healing, not additional bruises. The healing begins when I encounter someone who does not judge or condemn me, who does not ridicule or chastise me, who does not walk away from me or classify me as scum. The healing begins when I encounter someone who simply accepts me, listens to my story, and is willing to accompany me in the life I find myself in. Often it is a life without any joy or satisfaction, but it is a life that I have been entrapped in.

All of a sudden it was very clear what I had to do. I should simply befriend these people who walked the streets....

Carmen was a bit older, but a very beautiful woman. There was an incredible charm and dignity about her. Her husband had been from a very rich family in Mexico and she had come from a very poor family in Mexico. They had been married a few years and had three beautiful children. His family had never approved of their marriage. He died suddenly.

During the wake, she overheard his family conspiring as to how they were going to take the children away from her and chase her out on the street. She simply did not belong to "our class" and the children would be far better off without her. After all, they were very young and would be told that both of their parents had died early. They would never know about her or her lowly status.

She was deeply troubled, in desperation, and totally confused. Immediately after the funeral, she took the children and fled to a friend's house. She was frantic and had no idea what to do. She went to the basilica [of Our Lady of Guadalupe] to ask the Virgin for a miracle. On the way out, a woman stopped her and asked if she would be interested in well-paying employment in the United States. Of course! What kind of work? Entertainment, being a social hostess at events, accompanying people. It sounded great. The miracle had come quickly. The woman was even willing to give her a substantial cash advance and give her time to work things out and even arrange for her passport to the United States.

Through her friends, she was able to get her children into a Catholic school in a small rural town away from Mexico City. She made all the arrangements quickly and was soon on her way to New Orleans. She was full of excitement and expectation. Little did she suspect what was in store for her.

It was a totally different story when she arrived. Her passport was quickly taken away from her, she was housed in a prison-like place and instructed on the duties of her new job: to render sexual favors to the men who came around. There was no doubt, this was a high-class place and there would be good money involved, the money she needed to educate her children well. She hated the life she was entering into, but it was the necessary sacrifice for the sake of her children. It was horrible at first, but she learned to distance herself emotionally from her work; it soon became no different from sewing clothes in a sweat shop or picking crops in the fields, except the pay was much better and this enabled her to take good care of her children and even provide for her aging parents.

When she became older, she was dismissed. This was the only work she knew. She had traveled through several cities and ended up in San Antonio. She was very proud of her children and showed me treasured pictures of them. They had no idea what she was doing, but loved her visits when she would take them many gifts and clothing from the United States. I'll never forget some of her comments: "I did not choose this life; life chose it for me." She was not proud of her work, she lived in deep shame, yet she was proud and grateful that she still had her children, that her children had not been taken away from her, that she had given them a good education, and that they would never have to work at the type of work she had been forced into....

I would often end the day by spending time with the Lord in the Blessed Sacrament. He is very real to me. Often my stories did not have happy endings. There were many tragic ones. But I kept hearing his voice telling me: "I didn't succeed too well at first, they even abandoned me at the end, so just stay in there, keep loving them, and loving them even more."

It seems incredible to me that the more we advance in our world, the more fragile our world seems to become. Upward mobility seems to lead to personal disintegration while misery, abandonment, and poverty equally destroy the human spirit. We are indeed rushing to perfect the modern culture of death! Great capital is made at the cost of cheating the people and impoverishing the masses. Modern technology deprived more and more people of decent work. The contradictions are legion. Great and even miraculous medical advances are made at the same time as more and more people are denied even the most basic medical benefits. More and more crops are produced while more and more of the world's people die early because of starvation. Billionaires multiply while poverty enslaves millions.

Yet the great miracle is not that we believe in God. Who else can we go to that still has credibility? The great miracle is that God still believes in us! We do so many crazy, stupid, irrational things, and yet God keeps believing in us and calling us to build a better world. There is no time to waste. We are, all of us, called to walk with God in our homes, in public, in the workplace, and, yes, on the streets.

— "On the Streets of a Fragile World," 47–51, 54–55

DISCIPLESHIP

One of Virgilio's fundamental tenets about the human condition — in theological terms what one would call an effect of original sin — is our tendency toward divisiveness. It is not just that we tend to fear or distance ourselves from those whom we perceive as different from us. An even greater fault is our insecurity about our God-given worth and goodness independent of a comparison with another person or group we deem inferior. How often do we humans try in vain to bolster our own low esteem through demeaning one another! This fault is evident not just in ethnic and race relations, but in group dynamics ranging from high school cliques to the exclusive social clubs of adults. In the following passage, Virgilio presents Gospel dynamics that can animate Mexican American mestizos in their struggle for identity and a sense of dignity and belonging in a divisive world. The selection unveils the contours of a way of following Christ forged in the Mexican American experience of living between cultures, but it also inspires many others to walk the pathway of discipleship from the marginal Galilees of our world to our own Jerusalem confrontations with injustice.

"God chose those whom the world considers absurd to shame the wise" (1 Cor. 1:28)

It is in the very cultural identity of Jesus the Galilean and in his way from Galilee to Jerusalem that the real ultimate meaning of our own [*mestizo* Mexican American] cultural identity and mission to society become clear.

For those who ordinarily have a good sense of belonging, the idea of being chosen is nothing special. But for one who has been consistently ignored or rejected, the idea of being noticed, accepted, and especially chosen is not only good news, but new life. For in being chosen, what was nothing now becomes something, and what was dead now comes to life. In the light of the

Judeo-Christian tradition, our experience of rejection and marginalization is converted from human curse to the very sign of divine predilection. It is evident from the scriptures that God chooses the outcasts of the world not exclusively but definitely in a preferential way. Those whom the world ignores, God loves in a special way. But God does not choose the poor and the lowly just to keep them down and make them feel good in their misery. Such an election would be the very opposite of good news and it would truly be the opium to keep the poor quiet and domesticated. God chooses the poor and the marginalized of the world to be the agents of the new creation.

The experience of being wanted as one is, of being needed and of being chosen, is a real and profound rebirth. Those who had been made to consider themselves as nothing or as inferior will now begin to appreciate the full stature of human beings. Out of the new self-image, new powers will be released, powers which have always been there but have not been able to surface. Through this experience, the sufferings of the past are healed though not forgotten, and they should not be forgotten. For it is precisely out of the condition of suffering that the people are chosen so as to initiate a new way of life where others will not have to suffer what the poor have suffered in the past. When people forget the experience of suffering, as has happened to many of our immigrant groups in this country, such as the Irish in Boston, then they simply inflict the same insults upon others that had previously been inflicted upon them. The greater the suffering and the more vivid the memory of it, the greater the challenge will be to initiate changes so as to eliminate the root causes of the evils which cause the suffering. It is the wounded healer, the one who has not forgotten the pain of wounds, who can be the greatest healer of society's illnesses.

It is in our very marginalization from the centers of the various establishments that we live the Galilean identity today. Because we are inside-outsiders, we appreciate more clearly the best of the traditions of both groups, while equally appreciating the worst from the situation of both. It is precisely in this double identity that we in effect have something of unique value to offer both. The very reasons for the marginalization are the bases of our liberating and salvific potential not only for ourselves but for the others as well. In a privileged way, God is present in the marginalized, for distance from the powers of the world is closeness to God. It is consistently in the borderland regions of human belonging that God begins the new creation. The established centers seek stability, but the borderland regions can risk being pioneers. It is the borderland people who will be the trailblazers of the new societies. "The stone which the builders rejected has become the keystone of the structure. It is the Lord who did this and we find it marvelous to behold" (Matt. 21:42).

"I have chosen you to go and bear much fruit"
(John 15:16)

God chooses people not just to make them feel good, but for a mission. "I have chosen you to go and bear much fruit" (John 15:16). To accept God's election is not empty privilege, but a challenging mission. It is a call to be prophetic both in deeds and in words. It is a call to live a new alternative in the world, to invite others into it, and to challenge with the power of truth the structures of the world that keep the new alternative from becoming a reality.

Our Mexican American Christian challenge in the world today is not to become like someone else — Mexicans or Americans — but to combine both into a new way. It is through the very mechanisms of forging a new and more cosmopolitan identity that new life begins to emerge. It must be worked at critically, persistently, and creatively, for the temptation will always be there to become simply one or the other of the previous models. The temptation will always be there to restore the kingdom rather than to usher in the kingdom of God. In our present powerlessness we may think that this is stupid but, in our faith, we know that we must take the risks and begin to initiate new ways of life that will eliminate some of the dehumanizing elements of the present one. We know that we will not eliminate them all, nor will this come about easily and without much effort, organization, and frustration, but nevertheless the efforts must be made to introduce new forms and new institutions that will continue some of the best of the past while eliminating some of the worst. We will not build the perfect society, but we must do our part to at least build a better one. We must begin with the grassroots, but we must equally go to the very roots of the problems.

This is our "divine must"! We, too, must harden our faces and go to Jerusalem. We must go to the established centers of power, whether political, economic, educational, or religious, to confront their sacred idols that prevent them from truly serving all the people. It is the idols of society that function in favor of the rich and the powerful and against the poor and powerless. It is they that mask the hidden viciousness and manipulations of the wise of the world who find many ways of exploiting the poor and the simple of the world.

We really do not have a choice if we want to be disciples following Jesus on his way to the cross. It is this road from Galilee to Jerusalem which has to be continued if evil is to be destroyed, not with new forms of evil, but with the power of truth in the service of love. We have no choice but to speak the truth that brings to light clearly the evil of the world.

— "*Mestizaje* as a Locus of Theological Reflection," 371–73

UNMASKING THE IDOLS

Christian disciples are called both to do good and to resist evil. This entails our attempts to imitate Jesus' opposition to sinful human structures and tendencies. Early Christian missionaries to the "New World" of the Americas did not hesitate to condemn as idolatrous the gods and religious traditions of the natives. Five centuries later, in an invited lecture given in Rome to mark the anniversary of Columbus's 1492 voyage, Virgilio responded in kind, traveling to the "Old World" to offer the following reflections on the false idols of contemporary life, particularly in Western cultures.

Who is considered to be a good, beautiful, honorable human being in our society today? Who are the secular saints and heroes whom we look upon as the models of humanity? Who are the young people of our society striving to become?

What are those false idols that we in the West have created and worship, having eyes that see not, and ears that hear not? Are we worshiping the image and likeness of gods that we have created or are we open to being redeemed in the image and likeness of the God who created us, the God we meet in Jesus?

The First Idol: Money

The first idol I would like to identify is the conviction that the more one obtains in life the more one is. One of the unquestioned convictions in our society is that the fundamental human worth of a person is measured in terms of what the person has obtained. Those people are worth a lot, we say. Look at their car! Look at their clothes! Look at their homes! People measure human worth by possessions.

Whatever we have is linked to upward mobility. It seems to me that we are at a moment when we have to question the limits above which upward mobility is no longer good but destructive. Are there limits in upward mobility beyond which one becomes a public sinner and a social criminal? In the United States more and more people are unemployed, factories are being closed, and entire families suffer. I read in the *Wall Street Journal* the listing of the top ten salaried CEOs in the country. The first person on the list makes a salary of 92 million dollars per year. When people are unemployed, when some are destitute and starving, when more and more are having less, and fewer are having more and more, should we not ask what quantity of possessions make someone a public sinner?

We have to question this in our catechesis. We owe it to our people to tell them the truth. God has given the world for all God's people. Creation is beautiful. If some people work hard they should have the right to own their home and their land. On the other hand, some have so much when others do not have the minimum! Latin America is not poor. Latin America is rich! The scandal is there are so many poor people there. Have we ever questioned beyond what limits the possession of this world's goods is a public sin? One of the principles of the old moral theology was that if someone has more than he or she needs, and another does not have the minimum needed to survive, the one who has nothing has the right to go in and take what they need. We need to look at this basic reality in our moral theology.

Reading the incredible scandal stories in the newspapers one has the impression that everybody is out to make more money, no matter how they make it. A few months ago I read about an insurance scandal. The company was hiring very handsome, likable young men, the kind that any elderly woman would want to have as a grandchild. They would go to visit retirement homes and visit with elderly women and offer to sell them an insurance policy. Almost all bought a policy. The young men were insuring the elderly women in their sixties, seventies, and eighties for pregnancy risks. It was totally immoral but perfectly legal. Many such schemes are going on right now throughout the world. Balloon loans are made to people who buy homes. Suddenly the mortgage triples and they cannot pay it. The principle is to make a quick profit. It does not make any difference how you make it.

Another scandal emerged recently at the corporate level. It is too expensive to get rid of contaminated waste products in the First World so we send them to the Third World. Not only are we devastating the natural resources of the Third World, we are now making it a dumping ground for the contaminated trash that we find too expensive to decontaminate and take care of in our own land.

I remember how scandalized I was when I read several years ago that in an effort to "clean Brazil" of indigenous peoples, contaminated clothing was sent there from hospitals in the First World. Native people wore the clothing, contracted disease, and died. That was in the 1930s. But we are doing the same thing today; we are sending waste products there. We are testing drugs in the Third World, selling drugs and pharmaceuticals that are totally prohibited in the First World. The Third World has no controls; they are being used as human laboratories for profit making. Upward mobility? Make money? Profits for the country? We are fumigating crops in the United States while those who are picking the crops are in the fields, and their children are dying early of cancer. The reason remains the same — the profit motive. Is that the supreme value?

We, too, as religious persons have to question ourselves. How often have we fallen into profit-making schemes because we want to make our religious institutions bigger and better? How often have we used manipulative fundraising and maybe overused a mission in Africa or in Latin America to raise money and make our own congregations or institutions bigger and better? We fall too easily into believing that we need what is bigger and better.

We also need to question the sports heroes, the singers, and the entertainers who are making mega dollars through the support of poor people. Why should our sports figures make millions of dollars from poor people who go to see them play and not in turn subsidize sports so that the poor can play? Why do singers horde the money they make instead of building music schools in the poor districts, the urban districts, where children can learn music?

We have to challenge the rich, to ask whether having more makes one really better or whether having more makes one more satanic. We have to call it what it is in order to deal with it. It is the poor who are calling us to believe that in giving and sharing one receives the truth of the Gospel.

Come to our Cathedral of San Fernando in San Antonio, Texas. You will find a church of poor people. The liturgies have life, have real authentic joy because people are not playing games. They are giving to each other what little they have. It is in giving and not in taking that one becomes fully human. We need to recapture and share this fundamental truth of the Gospel.

The Second Idol: Pleasure

The second idol that I would like to explore with you is the conviction that pleasure brings happiness. Ours is a pleasure-seeking society. We are attracted to anything that will give us pleasure. Even with the current AIDS epidemic the majority of the population is not questioning its views on sex. They are simply saying that you have to be careful. People are not even questioning the fact that sex and drugs are destroying their families. Why do they look to sex and drugs for pleasure? The response is: Well, I was feeling down. I needed a pick-up. I felt rejected. I needed something to make me feel good.

High school students drop out of school. Why? I didn't like it. It wasn't fun. I wasn't enjoying it. The conviction is that if I am not enjoying it, it is not good. I have talked to couples who are thinking of divorcing. They have no serious reasons. The only reason is that they do not enjoy themselves anymore. The principle is that only pleasure brings happiness and, therefore, they have to be constantly entertained. This affects sports, music, school, church. Notice how often in our world people give as a reason, "I do not enjoy it."

What is happening? There is an increase of suicides. I remember many years ago being told that in counseling if young children tell you that they are going to commit suicide not to worry because they are not going to do it. It is different now. I recently received a cable from the parents of a young man.

They had gone to a prayer meeting, and when they returned home they found their son had hanged himself. He left a note saying that he was not enjoying life! — so why continue it?

The level of depression in our First World is incredible. I hear this from professional people in high positions. People simply give up. There is anxiety because they cannot have a good time. We need to question this, to rediscover that suffering is part of happiness, that continued pleasure does not lead to happiness.

There is a profound fundamental truth that we need to deal with: that happiness is realized only when one gives oneself to something that has meaning. This is the whole notion of service in the Gospel, the call to serve even in the smallest of things. Sacrifice for the sake of others leads to happiness. We must unmask the notion that pleasure brings happiness, that if you just enjoy what you are doing you will live happily ever after.

The Third Idol: Beauty

The third idol that we need to question is our concept of the beautiful. Who is considered a beautiful human being today? Just reflect on the advertisements that you see on television or in magazines. Look at what is projected as the image of the desirable human being. The image of the beautiful person that we in the First World are projecting as normative carries with it the message that if you are not this type of person you are not okay.

We project as beautiful the white, Aryan type. Look at the features. Those who fit the norm are tall, slim, not too old, not too young, well-built; they have perfect teeth, a perfect nose, perfect ears, perfect hair, perfect feet, the right smell, the right clothing. How we are regulating beauty!

There is much concern about diets. It is very important to discover the proper diet. I am not against dieting, but think about the extremes. More and more people suffer from anorexia. Children in grade school go through traumatic experiences because they are too fat and others make fun of them.

People spend hours exercising, dieting, not relating to their children, not relating to each other, not visiting, not having time to listen or to be aware.

Plastic surgeons today make more and more money remaking noses, chins, cheeks, and breasts. People are afraid of the human being that God has made them to be. We dare not look at ourselves in the mirror, without our toupee, our false teeth, our false arm, or whatever. We are afraid to say: "You know, God, you really outdid yourself when you made me the natural beauty that you made me!" When was the last time you thanked God for being the beautiful person you are? And just like you are?

All of us worry — and children to an incredible degree. If they are not white their trauma is unbelievable. A brown skinned co-student of mine from New Mexico recently told us something he had never admitted before. He used to wear long sleeves in his childhood because less of his skin would show! In the bathroom, he would spend hours rubbing himself with pumice stone trying to get "the dirt" out of his skin because he was brown.

What are we telling people? Poor children in San Antonio cannot afford braces for their teeth but are told that if they do not have perfect teeth they are not beautiful human beings. When my little kids at the cathedral come up to Communion a lot of them have teeth all over the place! Their parents cannot afford braces, but on the [more affluent] north side of San Antonio there is hardly a single kid without braces.

So the poor cannot afford to make themselves beautiful. Their added anxiety is that they have to accept the fact that society considers them ugly. No one wants to be ugly. Beauty has been literally reduced to externals — size, shape, clothes, jewelry. Only those that can afford it can be beautiful. All others are relegated to the world of the silent suffering of ugliness.

A girl I was working with tried to commit suicide recently. She comes from a small, very racist town. Her mother headed a one-parent family and had to work very hard to keep the family together. She did not have time to take care of herself. She was overweight, not because she ate too much, but because she could not afford the proper diet. The girl had a school invitation for her mother to attend parent-teacher meetings but she did not want her to go. She was embarrassed because her mother was dark skinned, heavy, and did not dress properly. She was not as good looking as the other mothers. In time she began to think she herself would become just as "bad" looking as her mother. Because of the pressures of beauty pageants in school and dressing right, this young girl, a junior in high school, tried to commit suicide. Do not underestimate the suffering of people and the pain when beauty is only seen as external.

We have to rediscover the inner beauty of the human being. This has to be the subject of our catechesis, our preaching, and our teaching — the inner beauty of each and every human being because each person radiates the beauty of God.

We need to rediscover that authentic, radiating beauty is the goodness of persons, how they give themselves to others, relate to others. At Communion in the Mass I love to see the beautiful callused hands of someone who has worked hard to bring up a family. I love to see the wrinkled faces of elderly Mexicans who have withstood the summers and the winters of life.

"One to one" relationship is rare among the poor. They do not have time for it. People do not teach them; people do not listen to them; people do not instruct them or take time just to be with them. To be with someone is to appreciate that person's beauty and dignity and worth. Today we must teach the truth of the beauty of the whole person; otherwise we will keep on trying to make ourselves more beautiful in ways that in effect destroy us.

The Fourth Idol: Power

The final idol I would like to unmask is that of violent power. It is seen as the source of honor and glory.

I was recently at a Third World theologians' meeting in Nairobi, Kenya. Dr. Takatso Mofokeng, a theologian from South Africa, mentioned how in his early days he had rejected Christianity. He felt so antagonistic when he heard hymns and songs of the type "all honor and praise and glory to thee, Redeemer King," for the very people who were oppressing him, denying him his existence, and putting him in jail were justifying themselves through this Christ of glory and power. He came to a moment when he even cursed Christ, because this Christ appeared to be justifying his own oppression and that of his people. It was in jail that he started to read the simple Gospel stories. It was there, he said, he discovered power and glory on his own — not the triumphalistic power that appeared to justify worldly power — but the real, ultimate power of the saving God in the powerlessness of Jesus of Nazareth. We need to unmask the way we identify the power and glory of God with the power and glory of this world's violence.

We are developing more and more effective weapons of war. Third World countries are given loans to acquire "weapons of defense"! The glorification of violence is destroying us. Our people are interiorizing the idea that the normal response to a stressful situation is violence.

In the United States, domestic violence has reached its highest level. Statistically speaking, the most dangerous place for a woman to be at night, the place where she is the most likely to be beaten up and hurt, is not in a bar, the street, or a dance hall, but at home with her husband.

Violence in our schools is phenomenal. The latest statistics seem to indicate that many children now take guns to class at some time — not play weapons but real guns. We have interiorized the understanding that the normal response to a stress situation is to kill. It happens at the domestic level, at the level of sexual differences, at the level of war games, and at the level of international politics. When we are threatened — send in the army!

I was personally horrified at the U.S. reaction to the 1991 Iraq crisis. I do not know what it was like in Europe but our people sat there, watching television and cheering as if the war were a game. No one asked how many were being killed nor about the suffering. We still have not been told how many were killed or buried alive. It was "a very clean war" from our perspective and we looked upon it as another video war game. Where are the heroes in this? Look at our movies and the glorification of ugly, destructive violence. The image given is that the more violent you are the more human you are.

We need to question the new world order that we are entering. So often the mind-set is that if you do not like something — attack! The great heroes — Gandhi, Martin Luther King, Jr., Archbishop Romero, Ita Ford, Jean Donovan, Dorothy Kazel, Maura Clarke, the Jesuit martyrs in Salvador with their house staff — all worked for peace in different ways. And they were all killed.

I recall a priest, a classmate of mine who was killed some years ago in Guatemala because he was labeled as subversive. He was teaching people how to farm and how to read and write. This was not acceptable to the forces of law and order in Guatemala, and so he was killed.

I recall a statement made by Archbishop Romero: "My love for my people is greater than my fear of death." When he was asked whether he should have guards to protect him, he said: "No! No, if God wants me to have the ultimate privilege of being a martyr, that will be God's praise, but my love for my people is all I have."

There are prophets like Dom Helder Camara and Dom Pedro Casaldáliga today in Brazil. There is the great Latin American theologian Gustavo Gutiérrez, a man who has known suffering in the most incredible ways. He speaks always about the God of life, about the Paschal mystery, and about finding new ways to eliminate violence. This is not the way of a world which prepares for peace by preparing for war! This is the way of

Jesus. Our world today needs prophets of peace to unmask the fragility and the falsity of the myth that weapons of war will lead us to peace.   — "Unmasking the Idols," 132–37

CONFRONTING COMMUNAL FAULTS

Complementary to his commentary on the defects of Western cultures, Virgilio has penned various passages like the following critique of what he perceives as some collective faults among Mexican Americans that can inhibit them from living the fullness of the Gospel message.

We must not limit ourselves to confronting the *others* with their faults against *us.* This would be easy and would quickly win us the acclaim of our own people, for we all like to hear how good we are at the expense of how bad the others are. This is true racism: to see oneself as essentially good while seeing the other as essentially evil. We must, as followers of Jesus, confront evil *wherever* its dehumanizing and disfiguring power is at work. This means confronting the evil ways not just of the others, but likewise of our own people.

It is true that the dominant society of both Mexico and the U.S.A. has treated Mexican Americans unjustly, and these injustices must be denounced as sinful, or even diabolical. However, we Mexican Americans also destroy ourselves from within. There are many beautiful aspects of our Latin American Catholic culture. But like all human cultures, it too is impregnated with sin — sin that becomes so ordinary that we fail to perceive it as destructive of life itself.

The Mexican American poor have to challenge the Latin American rich to be more responsive to the needs of the poor. In this, we have much to learn from our Calvinist brothers and sisters for whom wealth was a sign of blessing but also of social responsibility. The great problem posed by the Latin American rich is that for them wealth appears only as a blessing, not also as a responsibility. They easily and without any qualms of conscience squander their money on trips, jewelry, cars, sumptuous meals, and palatial homes while ignoring and exploiting the poor of their society. They despise the poor and ignore their misery.

There is hardly any *social consciousness* among wealthy Latin Americans. They see themselves "superior" by nature and not responsible for the misery of "inferior" human beings. There are no Latin American family foundations for the financing of social projects. They must be challenged. The Gospel must be announced clearly by the Latin American poor so as to liberate the rich from their empty and artificial lives that are being wasted away in the process of their own damnation.

There is a great sense of national and cultural pride and unity among us Mexican Americans, but we cannot unite for common projects. Our indomitable individualism and absolutism destroy our common efforts. Each one of us insists on having the last word and there is no room for compromise. If someone compromises, he or she is considered a "sell-out" — *un vendido*. It is noteworthy that there is no word for "compromise" in Mexican American Spanish. We do not need the Anglo or anyone else to divide us, for we quickly and easily divide ourselves and rip each other apart. As long as we can keep blaming the Anglo society for all our misfortunes, we will never advance. The truth is that there is evil on both sides — in the dominant group and in ourselves. But it is much easier to blame the other than to face ourselves. To face our limitations openly is essential to liberation. This works both ways, for the dominant society would likewise prefer to put the entire blame on the poor, the marginalized, and the foreigner rather than admit that they themselves are largely to blame for the sufferings of those living in misery.

Our beautiful Indian trait of indirect communication can degenerate into an obstacle to communication. Often we Mexican Americans are so overcareful about not offending the other that we never say what needs to be said. Thus at meetings we all agree with each other — but cut each other's throat as soon as we leave the session. Without losing that deep personal strength that allows us to be gentle and calm even in the most trying and difficult circumstances, we must learn how to disagree openly with each other without taking personal offense. We must learn that we can disagree without being disagreeable.

Our deep sense of honor and family unity sometimes leads us to unrestrained vengeance. If someone in our family has been offended, we are convinced that we have a blood obligation to avenge that person's honor. This leads to family feuds, fights, and murders. Our usual politeness and warmth can quickly turn into unsuspected forms of violence.

— *Galilean Journey,* 108–9

FESTIVE PROPHECY

As followers of Christ, even as we denounce evil and struggle to uproot it, we must bear in mind that ultimately God alone transforms minds, hearts, and the sin of the world. As we plod along toward God with our feeble efforts to be Christ's presence in the world, our joy and confident hope is that the Lord of the Universe races toward us from the end of history with a divine plan that no earthly power can thwart. Illuminating these convictions, in the following selection Virgilio explores the spirit of fiesta, a core feature of Mexican American life that is both the necessary partner of prophetic action and a participation in Christ's table fellowship of new life.

For prophecy to be truly Christian, it cannot stop at confrontation and denunciation. The fullness of Christian prophecy, which is not just the road to earthly Jerusalems but even beyond them to the heavenly Jerusalem, includes the festive celebrations of the inception of the heavenly Jerusalem here and now.

One of the greatest things the Christian has to offer our mixed-up and alienated world is that, while realistically facing the struggles of life, one can rise above them and experience and radiate authentic joy and hope, peace and serenity. It is in the celebrations of what has indeed begun but is yet to come in its fullness that the Christian announces the kingdom already in existence in our midst and nourishes the faith that enables followers of Jesus to endure even the cross.

The prophetic without the festive turns into cynicism and bitterness, or simply fades away. On the other hand, the festive without the prophetic can easily turn into empty rituals or even degenerate into drunken brawls. It is the prophetic-festive that keeps the spirit alive and nourishes the life of the group as a group. Moses was well aware of this when he commanded that the original and originating events of the Jewish people be celebrated annually. The Christian community was aware of it when it went on celebrating what had been most original in the way of Jesus: radical forgiveness that flowed into the joy of table fellowship with all persons. For living out this prophetic action Jesus had been crucified by human beings, but raised by God. In the joy of this heartfelt forgiveness that reintegrates the outcast into the community, the joy that comes with the awareness that you are accepted and valued simply because you are you, the Christians celebrated the death and resurrection of Jesus that brought about this new communitarian life transcending human frontiers and institutions. The celebrations of the originating events kept the group alive, thankful, and joyful even in the midst of the most cruel persecutions. There was a power in those celebrations that human powers could neither grasp nor destroy.

The joy of Mexican Americans is one of their most obvious characteristics. They love their fiestas and everyone is welcome to participate. Neither destitution nor wars can dampen their festive spirit. Even in the midst of suffering, there is a spontaneous joy that is not easily found elsewhere. Outsiders notice it and comment upon it. It is obvious in liturgical gatherings, spontaneous in home life, and carefully planned into commemorations of historical events. In their sorrows, disappointments, reverses, and struggles, there is joy. It is evident in the eyes and smiles of their children, in the playfulness of their youth, and in the inner peace and tranquility of their elderly. In the midst of whatever happens — triumph or tragedy — they rise above it to celebrate life.

It cannot be adequately explained but it can certainly be sensed, for it is nothing less than the joy of the experience of new life within them — not yet fully realized but certainly beginning.   — *Galilean Journey*, 119–20

PIETY

Virgilio emphasizes that Mexican Americans' religious fiestas and prayer traditions are a blessed means of encountering the God who accompanies them during times of mourning and joy, rejection and welcome, despair and hope, death and life. Their constellation of devotions is a living Creed for the faithful who pray them, even as those same devotions are constantly in need of evangelization and renewal in light of Scripture and tradition. The following excerpt from a presentation Virgilio gave to the U.S. Catholic bishops provides an overview of these treasured expressions of faith in the life of discipleship and in the life of the church, highlighting the core conviction that encountering Christ and his household of faith in prayer is foundational for knowing and following him.

Let us not deceive ourselves. A faith that is portrayed as highly rational, intellectual, and complicated cannot be the good news to the simple and lowly of society for whom it is primarily intended. Faith is not only a new body of knowledge as such, but a new relationship which allows me to cry out from the innermost depths of my heart, Abba Father. From this new relationship, new knowledge, new values, new rites, new heroes, and new forms of life will certainly follow. But no amount of knowledge, moral rigidity, or liturgical precision can substitute for the Spirit who alone transforms the heart from within. The most basic tenet of the church is God's self-revelation as the loving and intimate Mother/Father who invites us to experience ourselves as beloved children.

On this point, the Hispanic church has much to contribute to the entire community of believers. The popular faith expressions are the most beloved treasure of our people. They are also concrete manifestations of the church's tradition as it has been interiorized in the hearts of the faithful by the Spirit. These expressions begin to accomplish the goal of evangelization as the transformation not only of human hearts and the various strata of society, but even culture itself. Hence it should not be surprising that Paul VI told the Hispanic Catholics of the United States that we should not put aside our legitimate religious practices, nor that he told the entire world that popular piety manifests a thirst for God which only the simple and the poor can know.

If you will listen to our prayer forms, take part in our processions, devotions, and liturgical fiestas, listen to our ordinary first names, and see the decorations in our neighborhoods, homes, and even on our bodies, you will quickly discover that faith for us is not an abstract formula or merely a Sunday affair, but the fundamental living reality of our lives. In our devotion to the saints, the doctrines of our church are personalized and become human stories.

We meet Papacito Dios (Daddy God) from the earliest days of our lives, and God remains a constant source of support throughout life. We communicate easily and in a very personal way with God as Father, with Mary as our mother, with Jesus as our Lord and brother, and with the saints and souls in purgatory as members of our extended family. We argue with them, we ask them favors, we tell them jokes, we include them in our popular songs, we visit and converse easily with them. We keep pictures or images of them alongside the portraits of the family and best friends. We do not consider them graven images but rather simple expressions of our dearest friends. Their friendship is one of our deepest treasures and has enabled us to withstand the rejection of society without deep scars and to endure the suffering of oppression without giving up hope.

Yet our intimacy with them cannot be reduced to an opium that will drug us so as to keep us oppressed. The banner of Our Lady of Guadalupe has led all our struggles for justice — from the first struggles for [Mexican] independence to the present-day movements of the farm workers. She has been our leader and our strength. Mary has been our banner, the rosary has been our marching cadence, and the religious songs have been our invincible spirit.

Like Mary, we treasure in our hearts the revelations of Jesus as we have experienced him in the annual reenactment of the journey to Bethlehem in the *posadas,* the birth of Jesus, the visit of the shepherds and later on of the astrologers, the day of earth on Ash Wednesday, the *Semana Santa* (Holy Week) with the procession of palms, the washing of feet, the agony in the garden, the passion and death of Jesus, the *siete palabras* (seven last words), his burial and the *pésame* (condolences) to his mother, the Sabado de Gloria (Saturday of Glory) with the dramatic reenactment of the resurrection, May, the month of Mary, June of the Sacred Heart and Corpus Christi, October of the rosary, November of the communion of saints, all culminating with the great feast of Christ the King.

The first missioners, who planted the seeds of our *sensus fidelium,* were aware of the need to experience the fundamental elements of the mystery of Christ in a living way. For experience of Christ is the beginning of faith.

In these experiences of the historical events upon which the Creed is based, the people spontaneously intuit much of Christianity's deepest meaning. They may not be able to express it through the doctrinal formulation or theological discourse of the educated elite, but as you hear them speaking about what it means to them in their lives, as many of us experienced in the

Cursillo movement, there is certainly no doubt whatsoever that they truly intuit the deepest meaning of our faith....

Yet as positive a picture as I have painted, I am well aware that within our Hispanic community there is likewise imperfection, corruption, sin, and the need for growth and development. This is why we need the fellowship of the entire church. We need bishops with their theologians, priests, catechists, and other ministers who will share the same treasures of the heart which come through the intimate understanding of the spiritual things we experience together.

Preaching and teaching must arise out of the living reality of the faith, which is always historically and culturally conditioned. Otherwise, it will come across more as foreign imposition or a sort of religious ideology which will destroy people more than lead them to perfection. Thus we need pastoral agents who will not seek to put us down in the name of the Gospel but who will treasure the same culturally conditioned expressions of the faith, and in the light of Scripture and tradition purify and ennoble them so that they will more clearly express the glory of God.

— "The Treasure of Hispanic Faith," 205–6

LIBERATING PASTORAL LEADERSHIP

Virgilio does not limit his purview to his own experience and his own Mexican American people. He urges those of any background to join in solidarity with Mexican Americans and all those who struggle. The following selection from one of his first books offers his reflections for pastoral leaders who respond to God's call to accompany the suffering in a liberating way. In this early writing Virgilio deemed such pastoral leaders "oppressor-liberators" to denote the profound conversion they undergo in transcending dominant culture perspectives to listen, learn, and walk with the poor and the downtrodden.

Conversion to the oppressed requires a profound rebirth. Those who authentically commit themselves to the people must reexamine themselves constantly. The qualities of a true oppressor-liberator, one who truly wants to enter into the struggle for liberation, are trust of the oppressed and the ability to learn from them.

Those who are committed to the oppressed must have a willingness to trust the people's power to think, to know what they want, to seek their own destiny. The oppressed must be trusted enough to allow them to make some mistakes and gradually to learn how to analyze their own situation. They will never learn as long as someone else tries to do it for them; they must be trusted even when human instincts push the missioner to "do it for them just once more." They must be trusted, even when they seem incapable, as the Lord trusted his followers.

The poor are the teachers, and one must be willing to learn from the needs and aspirations of the poor. Whoever wants to work with the oppressed and the poor must learn to be a good listener. To be willing to learn from the poor is already *the first proclamation of the Gospel,* because learning from others is a very existential way of telling them that they are important and have something to offer. This affirmation of the fundamental dignity of the person is the beginning of rebirth unto liberation and salvation. To enter into true dialogue with those who have been rejected is to begin treating them as equals, and only from a position of equality can the liberation process make true progress.

The missioner must have a willingness to suffer with those he works with. The poor do not want pity from anyone, for it can be destructive. They do want compassion, someone to share their suffering and struggle so that from within the two may begin to work together for the liberation of both.

The poor are tired of having people want to do things for them; this can be dehumanizing. They are interested in having others do with them the things the poor themselves are convinced need to be done. As the new society begins to form, many persons are needed to help in its construction. Outsiders who want to join in the dialoguing process are most welcome, but outsiders who want to come in with their agendas, their answers, their way of doing things will turn out to be new oppressors; they are not welcome. The poor and the oppressed do not have a monopoly on the answers and the right way of doing things, but neither do the others; this is not a question of either/or, but one of true dialogue, an authentic search in which the oppressed and the oppressor-liberators join as equals in a true dialogue through which the correct way will gradually emerge.

A willingness to be patient is most important. Many times people are used to getting quick results. Often the poor do not know the many things that those in the establishment take for granted — the politics involved, the standard procedure to follow, the right person to see, the proper agency to deal with, and so forth. The learning process is not an easy one, and much patience and tolerance is needed. One of the constant temptations of the oppressor-liberator will be to do things for the oppressed.

As we have said, those who want to work with the oppressed must learn to depersonalize hurt. When there are frustrations and alienation, people tend to take it out on those closest to them; this also takes place in the apostolate. Often the many frustrations will be taken out on those who are the closest to the oppressed doing the most for them. The oppressor-liberator must learn that this is actually a sign of love, and is not an insult. It is a sad human phenomenon that people often take out their frustrations on those they love the most. It is not right, but it is the way people react. Learning to depersonalize hurt will be an asset to all who are committed to the process of liberation.

— *Christianity and Culture*, 146–48

JOY

One of the qualities Virgilio most appreciates in others is joy: not superficial happiness, but radiance rooted in the inner peace that comes from awareness of God's love and the satisfaction of serving God in our neighbor. This same quality is one that his friends deeply admire in him. In the following passage he pays tribute to the evangelical joy that marks the life of a longstanding friend and colleague.

Janie Dillard has been my close associate both at San Fernando Cathedral and at the Mexican American Cultural Center for many years.

Life has never been easy for her, yet she is the hardest working, most generous, and most joyful person I have ever met. When she was eight years old, her parents divorced, and her father abandoned the family. While her mother held two jobs to keep the family going, by the age of eleven Janie was already cleaning homes, doing laundry for neighbors, and working at other domestic jobs. When her mother died of cancer, a judge gave her legal custody of their household of three brothers and sisters even though she was only fourteen years of age. It was at that time, having dropped out of school to take care of her family, that she started working at a restaurant. She had learned early in life that you had a choice when bad things happened: let them destroy you through self-pity or allow them to make you stronger, better, and wiser. "I chose the latter," she says. This is the Janie I have come to know and admire.

Besides being very active in her parish, for many years she served as the volunteer assistant to Archbishop [Patricio] Flores in reaching out to poor people, helping them with food, utilities, and rent money, arranging for pauper funerals, helping with baby diapers, school clothing, and many other needs. Later on, she moved to San Fernando Cathedral to assist me with the many activities of a downtown church, one of which was welcoming the many street people who came by requesting help. She was always there, treating everyone with respect, dignity, and friendship. Janie was not only deeply involved in helping the poor and doing good for others; she was always conscious of her primary obligation as a wife, mother, and grandmother. She is truly a multitalented person who could easily have been a great success at any major enterprise, but she chose to live a simple life of loving service to others and in so doing she has found a deep sense of satisfaction and fulfillment.

—*Charity*, 15–17

CHARITY

Writings ranging from the biblical book of Job to Rabbi Harold Kushner's 1981 bestseller When Bad Things Happen to Good People *address "the problem of suffering," particularly the suffering of the innocent. Yet rarely if ever do we read about "the problem of compassion" or "the problem of charity." In the same way that we puzzle at how evil can be so widespread when a good God created the world, we do well to pause and wonder how human goodness and compassion often erupt from the most unexpected places, indeed, frequently from those very people who have suffered greatly. Virgilio's writings unveil such astonishing eruptions of Godliness, like the following meditation on charity that highlights the life of his friend and former archbishop, Patricio Flores, a migrant farm worker who went on to become the first Hispanic bishop in the United States and served as archbishop of San Antonio from 1979 to 2005. The selection opens with reflections on obstacles to charity like low self-esteem, envy, and the futile tendency to try to bolster our sense of self-worth through comparing ourselves to others. Such failings blind us to the true source of charity: our recognition that we are created in God's image and God loves us personally and infinitely. Discipleship like that exemplified in the life of Archbishop Flores entails a continuous meditation and renewal of the simple but transformative good news that when we accept God's gratuitous love, we in turn are set free to love.*

> "Disfigured by sin and death, man remains 'in the image
> of God,' in the image of the Son, but is deprived 'of the
> glory of God,' of his 'likeness.'"
>   — *Catechism of the Catholic Church,* no. 705

A son might physically be just like his father, but his behavior
might be totally different; hence one could say "you are the living image of your father, but you are certainly not like him at
all." Every human being, regardless of ethnicity, social class, or
even religion is created in the image of God, but not everyone
lives out the likeness of God, who is infinite love. In this reflection I'd like to explore some of the obstacles to love and some of
the deviations that I have experienced in my own life and in the
lives of others. We are all born into a world whose knowledge,
values, and priorities have been confused and sometimes totally
distorted by sin. Yet sin could not destroy the innate desires of
the heart that have been placed within each one of us by the creator. It is of the innermost nature of the human heart to desire
freedom, recognition, success, loving relationships, and happiness. Yet the big question is: How can we truly fulfill the desires
of the human heart?

I know there are many how-to books that offer to lead us to
fulfillment and happiness, and I have no doubt they offer very
good advice and have helped many people, but for the Christian
believer, the answer is quite simple: love!

> I give you a new commandment: love one another. As I
> have loved you, so you also should love one another. This
> is how all will know that you are my disciples, if you have
> love for one another. (John 13:34–35)

It is clear that love is the way to the fullness of life, but it
is not that easy to love, given our human condition. It is true
that we have been reborn in Christ and have begun the pilgrimage to eternal life, but between what has started in us and the
achievement of our final goal of eternal life in heaven there will
always be a large gap and a constant struggle. There are many

obstacles to the life of charity, but one of the roots of many of them is in our own insecurity due to our inadequate knowledge and appreciation of God and of ourselves. The ultimate basis of our infinite worth, dignity, and beauty is that we are created in the image of God, who is love, and our great challenge is to live out the likeness of God; the sadness is that because we lost the likeness of God, we don't recognize or appreciate ourselves or others for what we truly are. This leads to low self-esteem and self-centeredness in some while others might suffer from the opposite extreme with an exaggerated notion of their own dignity and self-worth. This can happen to persons as well as entire nations that fall into the idolatry of nationhood (*Catechism of the Catholic Church*, no. 57). A healthy self-knowledge and self-appreciation come from the proper relation between ourselves as creatures and God as our creator who created us in God's own image and likeness.

Low self-esteem is very painful and destructive and has many debilitating effects. It is a very lonely and isolated prison that conditions and limits much of our thinking and behavior. It keeps us from appreciating our own selves, from recognizing our abilities, and thus from even trying to develop the talents God has given us. When we are convinced that we are worthless, inferior, and incapable, we will not even try, and all the potential that is within us for doing good will be totally wasted, not because we are selfish but because we are convinced we have nothing to offer. Very painful consequences can easily flow from a low self-image, including envy, resentment, sarcasm, and even hatred. Yet it can also ignite a drive to succeed, to get ahead, to prove oneself. This is certainly good but can easily lead to the idolatry of success at any cost, hardening one's heart and sensibilities to the needs of others.

Envy and resentment destroyed the brotherly relationship between Cain and Abel and caused Cain to murder his brother. Ever since then it seems that rather than appreciating ourselves in our uniqueness we need to compare ourselves to others.

Rather than striving to become the best possible self, we struggle to become better than others. Envy can have many harmful consequences leading to self-destruction and the destruction of others. Many of the very popular Spanish-language *telenovelas* [soap operas] constantly bring out the disastrous consequences of envy as it leads to lies, intrigue, ugly gossip, betrayal, and even murder. When we are envious of someone, we allow that person to totally dominate our lives. We become blind to our own talents and possibilities because we are so obsessed with the talents and possessions of the other. Envy keeps us from discovering and appreciating our true self and often generates anger and frustration....

What gives us hope is the lives of the truly charitable persons who make an impact in our lives. In my parish, on the feast of All Saints, I invite the people to reflect with gratitude on the lives of those persons who have been saints to them, those who have touched their lives and made them better persons. When people reflect on this, it is truly inspiring to hear the many beautiful examples that come to mind. It might be the criminals who make the news, but we should never lose sight of the many saints that we have living among us, struggling with the many burdens of life yet enriching our lives and the lives of the entire community.

Charity is love in action. It is action on behalf of others arising spontaneously out of a loving heart, a heart that has experienced love and in a very special way has experienced the love of God, who is unconditional and unlimited love. These acts of benevolence are not looking for recognition or reward; they simply and very naturally flow out of the generosity of a loving heart. Nobody has to mandate them because they flow out of the deepest desires of a loving person. An excellent summary of love in action is found in the corporal works of mercy: to feed the hungry, to give drink to the thirsty, to clothe the naked, to visit the imprisoned, to shelter the homeless, to welcome the immigrant — especially the immigrant poor — to visit the sick, to bury the dead. These are the very activities, mentioned by Jesus in the Gospel according to St. Matthew (chapter 25), that will be the criteria for our final judgment. Jesus told us this not to scare us into doing good things, but rather to make us aware that it is in living out these activities that we discover the true meaning and purpose of human life. This is the way of life that leads to true fulfillment and integral well-being.

I am sure you have known many truly charitable people, but I would like to tell you about one for whom charity was always his most spontaneous response. The entire life of Archbishop Patrick Flores was one of constant charitable actions. I have many stories to tell about this charitable giant, but I will simply tell you about two incidents that exemplify the spontaneous and extraordinary charitable spirit of this man. One Saturday afternoon I dropped by his apartment for a visit. As I entered his room, he was paging through the telephone directory. I asked him who he was looking for. His response was that he had just heard in the news that a family's home had burned down, and he was looking for their address so that he could drive out to see them and offer them help. Most of us would have assumed that their family and neighbors would be there to help them, but Patrick Flores did not even stop to think who might help them, he simply said: "I am going to help them."

Another time a man broke into the chancery office, captured the archbishop, and held him captive for several hours while threatening to blow up the whole chancery office with a grenade. The chancery office was quickly evacuated and the entire city went into shock as police officers, FBI agents, law enforcement personnel, police cars, and even fire trucks surrounded the building while helicopters flew low over the area. The event quickly became a lead item in national and international newscasts. Friends from Europe and Latin America called to ask what was happening. Crowds of concerned people, young and old, surrounded the area and some were holding prayer vigils. Every minute that went by seemed like an eternity as tension and fear mounted.

Finally, around six in the afternoon, the man surrendered. The archbishop refused to press charges, but the state did. At the trial, the archbishop was called upon to testify by the prosecutor, but on the stand Patrick Flores argued in favor of his captor, stating that the man was not a criminal but a mentally sick person who needed help. He argued that the man should not be sent to jail but to a place for mental rehabilitation. The man was nevertheless convicted and sent to jail. At that point the archbishop began supporting the man's family, who were now left without financial support. I never heard the archbishop say anything negative about the man, and it was evident that he held no resentment. It made me think of the first word of Jesus from the cross: "Father, forgive them for they know not what they do" (Luke 23:34). One of the great manifestations of love is the ability to forgive not because we were not hurt, but because love is greater than any human offense.

I could give you many other examples from the life of this great man, whose guiding spirit was always the love of people and the desire to be of service to anyone in need. He traveled to Cuba to help in the release of political prisoners, to Eastern Europe and Latin America for relief services. He founded the National Hispanic Scholarship Fund (which today dispenses millions of dollars yearly in scholarships), and many other national and international works of mercy. But beyond all this, he was always there for anyone in need. He didn't ask any questions; he simply reached out with a helping hand and a loving heart. He was truly a living icon of the Good Samaritan. Now, in his retirement, he ministers by mail to people who are imprisoned for they too need to know that there is someone who still cares for them. This is the only way that rehabilitation will be made possible. Throughout his life, the corporal works of mercy have been the stuff of his everyday life.   — *Charity,* 61–64, 36–40

FORGIVENESS

One of the gravest obstacles to our transformation into new women and new men in Christ is the temptation to judgment and revenge that inhibits us from authentic reconciliation. How often the spirit of vengeance stifles joy and peace in our walk with Christ! All humans have suffered wrongdoing and we all face what seem like insurmountable difficulties in fulfilling the divine mandate to forgive as God has forgiven us. The following selection presents Virgilio's reflections on our call as disciples to imitate Christ's freedom to forgive his offenders. Consistent with his core insights on the Galilean Jesus' triumph over vengeance in his way of the cross and Our Lady of Guadalupe's reconciling presence to both conquerors and the conquered, this beautiful meditation integrates several strands of Virgilio's spiritual writings to address what is arguably the most vexing challenge of the Christian life: forgiveness.

In this world where sin, confusion, and perversion continue to reign in so many unsuspected ways and through so many masks of righteousness, justice, law, and order, the biblical assessment of humanity continues to be quite true: "There is no one who is righteous, no one who is wise or who worships God. All have turned away from God; they have all gone wrong; no one does what is right, not even one. Their words are full of deadly deceit...they are quick to hurt and kill: they leave ruin and destruction wherever they go. They have not known the path of peace, nor have they learned reverence of God" (Rom. 3:10–18). There seems to be no way out, for even in our quest for justice and reconciliation we often seek violence to avenge the debts or injuries inflicted upon us. The criminal has to be punished! The crime has to be avenged! The hurt honor has to be restored by bringing the other to his or her knees. It seems that only a violent punishment can compensate for a violent crime.

Often the only way we as humans think we can wipe out an offense is by offending the offender. If I have been offended, I continue to rage until the offender has received what I think he or she deserves. But even when the offender has received punishment, peace and tranquility are not yet forthcoming. The memory of the offense is still the source of anguish and turmoil. I still experience the bitterness or at least some disappointment. The resentment and the anger continue to rage within me. Frequently I will take it out on others without even realizing what I am doing.

The greatest damage of an offense — often greater than the offense itself — is that it destroys my freedom to be me, for I will find myself involuntarily dominated by the inner rage and resentment — a type of spiritual poison which permeates throughout all my being — which will be a subconscious but very powerful influence in most of my life. Often I will become irritable and insulting, difficult to get along with, and even malicious. I do not even recognize my own self. I begin even to hate my new self. I was not that way before, but I cannot help the feelings within me. I hate the offender for what he or she has done to me but in the very hatred of the other I allow that person to become the Lord and master of my life. Their life will become one of the dominant forces controlling my entire life. What is God waiting for? Why doesn't God hurry up and punish them?

Can the Jews forget the Holocaust? Can the Japanese forget Nagasaki and Hiroshima? Can the prisoners of war forget the German concentration camps? Can the Native Americans forget the European invasion, conquest, genocide, and domination? Can the blacks of the Americas forget their generations of enslavement?

Can the child forget the beatings by an alcoholic parent? Can a spouse forget the infidelity of a spouse? Can a friend forget the betrayal of a friend? Can a student forget the ridicule of a teacher? Can a worker forget the dehumanizing insults of a supervisor? No matter how much one wants, no one can uncreate the past. What has happened has happened. We have to live with it; we have to cope with it; we cannot undo it; we can never completely wipe it out.

The deeper the hurt, the greater the controlling influence of the aftermath. It comes to the point when, as the scriptures say: "I cannot even understand my own actions. I do not do what I want to do but what I hate" (Rom. 7:15). Depression, anxiety, feelings of anger mixed with feelings of unworthiness and inferiority become part of my daily existence. Counseling, hard work, vacations, rest, medicine, group therapy — they all help but nothing seems to restore my inner freedom, self-acceptance, and peace. Must I simply adjust to living my life in misery, dominated by the very person who offended me?

The ultimate sinfulness of sin itself and its greatest tragedy is that it converts the victim into a sinner. The offended feel in the very entrails of their being the need to demand payment in kind. It seems that the damage done by sin can be repaired only by sinning against the one who sinned, except that the action taken against the offender appears as necessary according to the demands of justice. The culprit must be punished — must receive what he or she deserves. The sin must be avenged and, in avenging it, the victim now becomes the sinner for the victim has repaid an evil action in kind! Thus not only has one sinned, but the reaction has made a sinner out of the victim.

The great tragedy is that this type of retaliation simply contributes to the growth and development of the expanding spiral of violence. Furthermore, the scars made on the heart, the memory, and the very soul of the hurt person are themselves a type of spiritual cancer which will simply eat away at the life of the victims. This causes them to be what they do not want to be — grouchy, cantankerous, withdrawn, deceitful, aggressive, jealous, angry. "What a wretched person I am! Who can free me from this body under the power of death?" (Rom. 7:24). Humanly speaking, there seems to be no way out of the misery created by human beings.

Left to ourselves, repaying offense with offense, we would surely destroy ourselves for even when we have punished the offender, we are still cursed with the memory of the offense which brings out feelings of anger and disgust. Once offended, it seems that I will never really regain the peace, tranquility, and composure that existed before. Even when avenged, the cancer of the wounded heart is not healed but continues to eat away at the very life of the victim. Alone, we do not seem capable of rehabilitating ourselves. We appear condemned to misery for the rest of our lives; worst of all, we pass it on to successive generations in such ways that these types of retaliatory attitudes and actions become part of the historically developed functional nature of humanity. This mind-set becomes so deeply ingrained in our humanly developed ways of life that it not only appears and functions as natural but even as demanded by divine righteousness. Retaliation appears as a demand of nature and nonretaliation appears as weakness, cowardice, and even failure. We learn so well from previous generations and interiorize so deeply what we have received that now the very heart demands retaliation as the only way it will be healed.

No wonder that some Jewish leaders said Jesus was blaspheming when he forgave sins: humanly speaking, true and unconditioned forgiveness seems beyond our natural possibilities or even the deepest demands of the heart. To forgive is to wipe out the offense. To forgive means to uncreate, but since only God can create out of nothing only God can return to nothing what has already come into existence. So it is only God who can uncreate; it is only God who can truly forgive. Thus for men and women it seems that retribution is the only way to appease the pain created by the offense, yet retribution will never be full rehabilitation....

To believe in Jesus is the beginning of our rehabilitation. It is through my faith in Jesus that I am redeemed from the death traps of our ordinary ways. To believe in Jesus is to make his way our own and to follow in his footsteps, even when my flesh — my natural inclinations — pull in the opposite direction. The more we believe in Jesus, the more that his very life becomes our own life and "If Christ lives in you, the Spirit of

life is for you" (Rom. 8:10). This spirit crushes our sinful inclinations to revenge and vengeance. It is this spirit that brings
about, not just an adjustment in the self, but a total rebirth into
new life. "The Spirit of God makes you God's children and by
the Spirit's power we can cry out to God: 'Abba, my Father' "
(Rom. 8:14–15). It is this new life — the life of God's own life
within us — that allows us to go beyond our natural inclinations. In Christ, former values and needs are reversed: "For
those things which I used to consider as gain, I have now reap-
praised as loss in the light of Christ" (Phil. 3:7). And the true
justice of God now reigns in place of the justice of an unjust
humanity: "The justice I possess is that which comes through
faith in Christ. It has its origin in God and is based on faith"
(Phil. 3:9).

It is the belief in Jesus that regenerates us. It transformed Paul
from the zealous persecutor of those who disagreed with him to
the untiring apostle of God's unlimited and universal love for all
men and women. Even when he was persecuted, beaten, jailed,
and insulted, he continued to live and proclaim God's love and
forgiveness. Stephen died, like Jesus, with the words of forgiveness for his assassins. The early martyrs went to their death not
shouting curses or demanding justice but singing praises to the
God of life. In all these cases, a new peacefulness had taken
over. There was no burning desire for revenge and no righteous instinct crying for justice. Now, even if they were insulted,
maligned, and killed, they could no longer be destroyed. When
following our natural ways, even if we were not killed, we were
often destroyed by our own inner feelings and gut emotions
of anger, anxiety, hurt, disillusion, and disgust. We were condemned to a living death. But now there is a total reversal.
Nothing can destroy the inner peace and tranquility of someone
whose heart has been transformed from stone to love.

Thus in forgiveness, it is not a question of forgetting the
injuries or ignoring the hurt. In fact it is not even good to forget
because if we forget, we might easily repeat the same offenses

ourselves, and if we are not aware of the hurt, we could easily be ignorant of the incredible hurt that we are able to inflict upon others, even without realizing it. Remembering can be a great teacher and even a source of growth and development in our abilities to be sensitive to others. Hurts transformed by love can be the greatest source of compassion for the hurts of others. The painful memories of the offense, healed through faith in Jesus, can be the greatest sources for a very fruitful ministry of reconciliation among today's aching humanity.

The real challenge to humanity is not one of forgetting, but one of converting. It is in converting to the way of God through our encounter and subsequent faith in Jesus that we make the radical and definitive break with the natural ways of justice and begin to enjoy the justice of God, which in this life repays curse with blessing, injury with pardon, theft with gift, insult with praises, and offense with forgiveness. "To be controlled by human nature results in death; to be controlled by the Spirit results in life and peace" (Rom. 8:6). A new "natural law" begins to function and thus we no longer do what we are urged to do by the pull and pressure of our human customs and traditions but what we are empowered to do by the Spirit. It is not for us to judge or punish, for in the end it will be God who alone knows the secrets of the heart and who will dispense the true justice of the final judgment.

Forgiveness is love surpassing righteousness and divine mercy transcending human justice. Jesus freely accepted death rather than break his loving relationship with others — friends or enemies. Even though the cowardly actions of the apostles on the first Good Friday certainly merited his disgust and at least a good scolding, Jesus does not allow the betrayal by his followers to be the basis of his relationship with them. His love transcends the demands of the human yearnings of the fleshly heart. The first act of the Risen Lord is to go to the Apostles not to scold them or demand apologies, but to offer them total and unconditional *shalom*. Jesus will not allow their bad and stupid actions to be the basis of his loving relationship with them.

Belief in Jesus enables us to live as Jesus lived. When we are offended, although we are hurting, belief in Jesus and his way allows us to withdraw our disapproval of the offense, even though we have no doubt that it is warranted. We can do this willingly because we do not wish to make the offense the basis of the relationship between us. This does not mean that we approve or ignore the evil that has been done, but simply that we refuse to make the offensive action the basis of our relationship. Forgiveness is not understanding, nor forgetting, nor ignoring. It is an act of generosity that deliberately overlooks what has been done in order to remove the obstacle to our friendship and love. Jesus does not allow the merits or demerits of my life to be the basis of his stance toward me.

Forgiveness is not a consequence of justice, but an outflow of divine generosity toward us which is now alive in us. If God forgives, who am I, sinner that I am, to condemn others? The spontaneous sign that I have truly accepted God's forgiveness is that I will be able to forgive others as God has forgiven me. It is in the very forgiveness of others that I truly interiorize and make my very own God's forgiveness of me! In forgiving others, I ratify and make my own God's generous offer of universal forgiveness. Now I too can forgive as only God can forgive! Thus it is in forgiving that I am divinized: to err is human, to forgive divine!

In this way I die to the old self that cries out for understanding and restitution. The old demands of the fleshly heart decrease as the new life of the Spirit begins to take hold, grow, and mature within me. The more I am "grasped" by Christ, the more I will experience the fruits of the Spirit.

Forgiveness will never be easy, for the demands of the natural self will continue to be strong and nag us in many different ways. Yet it is certainly possible and even joyful and peace-producing when we dare to believe in Jesus and trust in his ways. By any human standard his ways will often appear to be senseless and unjust, yet they are the only way to break the destructive cycle of the offender who creates another offender out of the very person injured. To the degree that we trust our own ways rather than the ways of God, we will go on destroying ourselves and one another. The only way is to put our full confidence in the way of the Lord.

When we dare to trust the divine physician and accept his prescription, we will find ourselves restored to the fullness of human health, and even when we die, we will die in peace and sleep the sleep of the just.

— "I Forgive but I Do Not Forget," 70–72, 76–78

RISEN LIFE

This final excerpt comes from meditations and prayers created for a video production of the way of the cross. The selection concludes this anthology with Virgilio's prayer for those who walk the way of Christ.

Jesus invites you and me to "come and follow him." It is easy to follow him along the lakes and fields of Galilee, but it becomes more difficult as he enters Jerusalem, and most difficult as he walks under the weight of the cross unto Calvary. Yet he still invites you and me to come and follow along his very own footsteps. Let us accept his invitation together that we might continue to grow in the appreciation of his love for us and thus share in his power unto resurrection. . . .

O Risen Lord, help me to see
that even my greatest failures
are but opportunities of new beginnings.
You never gave up on loving us,
even when we rejected you unto the cross.
Help me, give me the wisdom and the courage
to be ever more creative in finding ways
of loving others as you have loved us.
Let me die to destructiveness
that I may live unto the creativity of new life.
Arise in me, that others might arise through me.
Amen.   — "San Fernando Cathedral's
                              Way of the Cross," 2, 9

Bibliography

Beyond Borders: Writings of Virgilio Elizondo and Friends. Ed. Timothy Matovina. Maryknoll, N.Y.: Orbis Books, 2000.

Charity. Maryknoll, N.Y.: Orbis Books, 2008.

"A Child in a Manger: The Beginning of a New Order of Existence." In *Proclaiming the Acceptable Year,* ed. Justo L. González, 64–70. Valley Forge, Pa.: Judson Press, 1982.

Christianity and Culture: An Introduction to Pastoral Theology and Ministry for the Bicultural Community. Huntington, Ind.: Our Sunday Visitor, 1975.

"Converted by Beauty." In *The Treasure of Guadalupe,* ed. Virgilio Elizondo, Allan Figueroa Deck, and Timothy Matovina, 73–78. Lanham, Md.: Rowman and Littlefield, 2006.

"Evil and the Experience of God." *The Way: Contemporary Christian Spirituality* 33 (January 1993): 34–43.

The Future Is Mestizo: Life Where Cultures Meet. 1988; rev. ed. Boulder: University Press of Colorado, 2000. Originally published in French: *L'Avenir est au mestissage.* Paris: Nouvelles Editions Mame, 1987.

Galilean Journey: The Mexican-American Promise. 1983; rev. ed. Maryknoll, N.Y.: Orbis Books, 2000.

A God of Incredible Surprises: Jesus of Galilee. Lanham, Md.: Rowman and Littlefield, 2003.

Guadalupe: Mother of the New Creation. Maryknoll, N.Y.: Orbis Books, 1997.

"Hispanic Theology and Popular Piety: From Interreligious Encounter to a New Ecumenism." *Proceedings of the Catholic Theological Society of America* 48 (1993): 1–14.

"I Forgive but I Do Not Forget." In *Forgiveness,* ed. Casiano Floristán and Christian Duquoc, 69–79. Edinburgh: T. & T. Clark, 1986.

"Jesus' Dying Words Give Us Life." *San Antonio Express,* April 4, 1995, 5B.

"Jesus the Galilean Jew in Mestizo Theology." *Theological Studies* 70 (June 2009): 262–80.

"Mary and Evangelization in the Americas." In *Mary, Woman of Nazareth,* ed. Doris Donnelly, 146–60. New York: Paulist, 1989.

Mestizaje: The Dialectic of Cultural Birth and the Gospel. 3 vols. San Antonio: Mexican American Cultural Center Press, 1978.

"*Mestizaje* as a Locus of Theological Reflection." In *The Future of Liberation Theology: Essays in Honor of Gustavo Gutiérrez,* ed. Marc H. Ellis and Otto Maduro, 358–74. Maryknoll, N.Y.: Orbis Books, 1989. Originally published in French: "Le mestissage comme lieu theologique," *Spiritus* 24 (December 1983): 349–75.

"The Mexican American Cultural Center Story." *Listening: Journal of Religion and Culture* 32 (Fall 1997): 152–60.

La Morenita: Evangelizer of the Americas. San Antonio: Mexican American Cultural Center Press, 1980.

"On the Streets of a Fragile World." In *Walking with God in a Fragile World,* ed. James Langford and Leroy S. Rounder, 47–55. Lanham, Md.: Rowman and Littlefield, 2003.

"Our Lady of Guadalupe as a Cultural Symbol: 'The Power of the Powerless.'" In *Liturgy and Cultural Religious Traditions,* ed. Herman Schmidt and David Power, 25–33. New York: Seabury, 1977.

A Retreat with Our Lady of Guadalupe and Juan Diego: Heeding the Call. Coauthored with five friends. Cincinnati: St. Anthony Messenger, 1998.

San Fernando Cathedral: Soul of the City. Coauthored with Timothy Matovina. Maryknoll, N.Y.: Orbis Books, 1998.

"San Fernando Cathedral's Way of the Cross through the Streets of San Antonio" (unpublished script for video production). San Antonio: Catholic Television of San Antonio, 1997.

A Search for Meaning in Life and Death. Manila, Philippines: East Asian Pastoral Institute, 1971. Reprinted as *The Human Quest: A Search for Meaning through Life and Death.* Huntington, Ind.: Our Sunday Visitor, 1978.

"Transformation of Borders: Border Separation or New Identity." In *Theology: Expanding the Borders,* ed. María Pilar Aquino and Roberto S. Goizueta, 22–39. Mystic, Conn.: Twenty-Third Publications, 1998.

"The Treasure of Hispanic Faith." *Origins* 10 (September 11, 1980): 203–8.

"Unmasking the Idols." *SEDOS* 24 (May 15, 1992): 131–40.

The Way of the Cross of the Americas. Maryknoll, N.Y.: Orbis Books, 1992.

ACKNOWLEDGMENTS

Excerpts from *A God of Incredible Surprises,* "Converted Beauty," as it appears in *The Treasure of Guadalupe,* and "On the Streets of a Fragile World," as it appears in *Walking with God in a Fragile World,* reprinted by permission of Rowman & Littlefield Publishers, Inc.

Excerpts from "Evil and the Experience of God," in *The Way: Contemporary Christian Spirituality,* reprinted by permission of *The Way.*

Excerpt from *Theology: Expanding the Borders,* reprinted by permission of the College Theology Society.

Excerpts from "Unmasking the Idols," reprinted by permission of SEDOS.

Excerpts from "The Mexican American Cultural Story," reprinted by permission of *Listening: Journal of Religion and Culture.*

Excerpts from *Mary, Woman of Nazareth,* reprinted by permission of Saint Mary's College.

Excerpts from "Jesus the Galilean Jew in Mestizo Theology," in *Theological Studies,* reprinted by permission of Theological Studies, Inc.

Excerpt from "The Treasure of Hispanic Faith" in *Origins,* reprinted by permission of Catholic News Service.

Excerpts from *The Future is Mestizo: Life Where Cultures Meet,* reprinted by permission of the University Press of Colorado.

MODERN SPIRITUAL MASTERS
Robert Ellsberg, Series Editor

Already published:

Dietrich Bonhoeffer (edited by Robert Coles)

Simone Weil (edited by Eric O. Springsted)

Henri Nouwen (edited by Robert A. Jonas)

Pierre Teilhard de Chardin (edited by Ursula King)

Anthony de Mello (edited by William Dych, S.J.)

Charles de Foucauld (edited by Robert Ellsberg)

Oscar Romero (by Marie Dennis, Rennie Golden,
    and Scott Wright)

Eberhard Arnold (edited by Johann Christoph Arnold)

Thomas Merton (edited by Christine M. Bochen)

Thich Nhat Hanh (edited by Robert Ellsberg)

Rufus Jones (edited by Kerry Walters)

Mother Teresa (edited by Jean Maalouf)

Edith Stein (edited by John Sullivan, O.C.D.)

John Main (edited by Laurence Freeman)

Mohandas Gandhi (edited by John Dear)

Mother Maria Skobtsova (introduction by Jim Forest)

Evelyn Underhill (edited by Emilie Griffin)

St. Thérèse of Lisieux (edited by Mary Frohlich)

Flannery O'Connor (edited by Robert Ellsberg)

Clarence Jordan (edited by Joyce Hollyday)

G. K. Chesterton (edited by William Griffin)

Alfred Delp, S.J. (introduction by Thomas Merton)

Bede Griffiths (edited by Thomas Matus)

Karl Rahner (edited by Philip Endean)

Sadhu Sundar Singh (edited by Charles E. Moore)

Pedro Arrupe (edited by Kevin F. Burke, S.J.)

Romano Guardini (edited by Robert A. Krieg)
Albert Schweitzer (edited by James Brabazon)
Caryll Houselander (edited by Wendy M. Wright)
Brother Roger of Taizé (edited by Marcello Fidanzio)
Dorothee Soelle (edited by Dianne L. Oliver)
Leo Tolstoy (edited by Charles E. Moore)
Howard Thurman (edited by Luther E. Smith, Jr.)
Swami Abhishiktananda (edited by Shirley du Boulay)
Carlo Carretto (edited by Robert Ellsberg)
John XXIII (edited by Jean Maalouf)
Jean Vanier (edited by Carolyn Whitney-Brown)
The Dalai Lama (edited by Thomas A. Forsthoefel)
Catherine de Hueck Doherty (edited by David Meconi, S.J.)
Dom Helder Camara (edited by Francis McDonagh)
Daniel Berrigan (edited by John Dear)
Etty Hillesum (edited by Annemarie S. Kidder)